Praise for *Never Young*

"This author's unique voice makes you feel like you can time-travel."

Jane Catherine Rozek, author of Girl Goes North

"*Never Young* is a fascinating memoir about growing up in a poor, rural area in Poland after WWII. The book is filled with harrowing moments of danger, heartbreak, and loss, as well as hope. Whenever young Krystyna seemed destined for harm, help arrived. Filled with fascinating detail and flawed, but loving people of faith, this is a book you'll recall long after you turn the final page."

Lynne Klippel, author of Overcomers, Inc.

"A gripping story of survival and faith. I can't wait for Book Two."

Michelle Barker, author of The House of
One Thousand Eyes

Acknowledgements

Thank you to my supportive husband, Lyle,
who believed in my story—
you are the wind beneath my wings;

to my sons, Collin and Trevor—
I love you;

to my brothers and sister—we have journeyed
together and have grown through pain;

and to my parents,
who are no longer here with us—I miss you.

Thank you also to my beta readers—Jane Rozek,
Susan De Beeson, Faye Cyr and Slavomir Almajan—
for their challenging suggestions;

to Norma Hill and Michelle Barker
for patiently editing my manuscript;

and to Dawn Renaud for helping me transform it
into a finished book.

PART I

❧ 1960 ❧

Chapter One

I have planned this escape in my mind a thousand times and here it is happening today. Everything is going to be perfect. I am filled with excitement, yet scared at the same time. The sun is shining on my back and I feel alive and free as I start walking. The road is very rough, with potholes and big rocks everywhere. My thin shoes are not sturdy enough, but they are the best I have and I am happy.

As I walk farther and farther away from my parents, I look forward to getting away. I am escaping to the city of Sosnoviec from my home in the village of Topola. Sosnoviec is about a day's journey by train through rural Poland, with cars and busses which I have never seen before.

I count the money once again and am sure I have enough for the ticket. For some time, I have been helping with some sewing at the seamstress's home down the road and she has given me a few pennies to save. My parents do not know. I don't want them to find out that I am working and learning something new instead of farming.

Saving pennies seems to be an impossibly long way to earn enough money for a train ticket. Now, suddenly, my prayers have been answered and I have enough. I am going straight home to pack my suitcase, and then I will go to the train station, and then I will escape.

My heart starts to pound with excitement, yet I am also afraid of disappointing my parents. They trusted me. They count on me to look after my younger brothers and pull weeds and help feed the animals. But I am putting all of that, and all of the nasty gossip about me and my friend Tomek, behind me now. This is my chance.

As I skip down the rutted road, singing some of the songs I have been gathering for my song book, I hear a wagon coming behind me.

"Get in the wagon," calls the driver as his horse begins to pull alongside me. "You will cook walking in this heat." When I turn to see who it is, the sun is shining in my eyes and I squint up at him. I blush at the way his gaze takes me in, starting with my hair tied up in pigtails and continuing downward to settle for a lingering moment somewhere in the midst of my body, and finally dropping to observe the hem of my worn dress and my old shoes.

Defiantly, I stand straighter and lift my chin. "No thank you. I am walking to Topola all by myself and I don't need a ride."

"At least get in the back of the wagon for a little ways," he suggests. "It is much too hot to be walking all that way."

Again I refuse, and again he insists. I begin walking and suddenly he jumps down, hoists me up, and pushes me into the back of the wagon, where I tumble onto my back. Climbing onto his seat, he proceeds to drive along the bumpy dirt road toward town.

From where I lie, winded and surprised, I stare up at him. He is unshaven, mostly bald with a few straggly strands of reddish-brown hair, and no front teeth. I wonder if he had them knocked out at the local bar, where most of the men hang out at night to drink and argue. Once I went to the bar with Mom to pick up my dad after he was drinking most of the day with his friends. I heard loud voices arguing with words I had never heard before. Mom told me to cover my ears and hum, and I did until she came back with Dad, who was very drunk. He was arguing with Mom and didn't want to go home until I calmed him down. I've had a calming effect on Dad from an early age. When we walked home together, Mom and I had to hold onto Dad to help him along.

This wagon has a layer of dirty, smelly straw with some dried-up blood on it, probably from hauling a butchered animal. The stink is curling my nose hairs, as my dad would say. I begin to pray, trying not to breathe deeply. Between prayers, I try to lose myself in thinking that soon I will be home and packing, and then I will be on the train.

It is Monday, June 27th, 1960, seven days after my eleventh birthday. We don't celebrate our birthdays, as there is never any money for things like gifts or birthday parties, and today started out like any ordinary Monday. School is now officially over for the summer months, and this means my brothers and I join our parents to work on the farm.

Pulling weeds is our daily routine. But this morning I had not been feeling well, even before we left our house at 5:30 to ride to the farm in Dad's wagon. We had been working for a few hours, and my little brothers, Stan and Jim, were running around pulling weeds and sometimes also pulling up some of the vegetables. Dad was getting agitated and yelling at them.

"Stop this nonsense or I will give you something to run around for. It is too hot to be doing this sort of thing. Get back to work." Then he turned his attention to me. "Krysia, how are you doing?"

"Not very well," I told him, wiping the sweat from my eyes. "Maybe I should go home. I am grown up enough to walk home by myself if I have to."

"All eight kilometers, on your own?" Dad looked at me with his half smile and said, "We'll see about that," as he walked away.

I live in Poland with my parents, my grandparents and two brothers in a rural town called Topola. The population is about 350, most with farms and orchards, and that sums it up. Almost everyone in town has a property outside of town, from which they make a living. Some folks have a much bigger piece of land while the rest, like us, make just enough to survive.

The people who live here all work very hard, and everyone is out in their fields from dawn to dusk, from early spring to late fall. No one stays home to babysit for others. A few families have an older great-grandma who cannot do farm work, so she looks after their small children. But most people must drag even their smallest children along wherever they go. It is our normal way of life.

In the summer, we can almost hear the heat crackle. At sunset the sky is like a sheet of fire. People suffer from this heat, but everyone stays late hours on their fields to accomplish just a bit more. That is the way for my parents and grandparents and everyone I know living here.

I have been preparing my dad for the time when I would be ready to go home and put into action my plan—my escape from Topola. I will need him to trust me enough to let me walk home from our farm field alone. I've reminded him that when I belonged to Girl Guides, I was able to survive a trip to another neighboring town and come back, all in the same day, safe and sound. And I'm older now.

I hope today will be the first time he would allow it. After that it will be easier to convince him to let me go. Dad is the one who will decide. My mom just goes along with what he says. She seems lost most of the time, mourning the loss of her last two babies. She is not well and tries to avoid any extra stress. If she disagrees with Dad, she knows it will just lead to an argument when they get home at night.

After another half an hour or so, Dad decided to send me home. I was pleased, just thinking this would be my first practice trip. But then Dad told me, "Since you are going to do nothing constructive anyways, you can go to the corner store and settle our account. The store will be closed when we get home, so you can help us that way." Everyone in our town purchases goods on credit, and when they sell something from the farm, they pay their account off until the next purchase. Dad handed me some money. "Don't lose it, as that is all we have."

I tried not to show my excitement as I looked down at the bills in my hand. Could it be that I actually had enough money now to put my plan into action?

As I started for home, Dad shouted after me, "You better not forget to peel the potatoes for our supper."

My family would be staying late on the farm, so I knew I had a lot of time to get packed and catch the next train. And now, even though it is not what I wanted, the wagon ride will get me home even sooner.

❧ ❦

The wagon is slowing down. We are about halfway to town, and down a short road off to the side there is a small creek and a big tree. It is the only tree to be seen for many kilometers. The driver says the horse needs to cool off, and it will be good for us to cool off as well.

Although it is still morning, the sun is baking us. In the summer months, it often gets very hot before noon, with very little breeze. The wild flowers look wilted on the side of the road.

I am desperate for a drink of water, and I get down from the wagon, pull off my shoes, lift the hem of my dress and step into the creek to wet my feet and my legs. But the driver doesn't move. He just sits there on the wagon bench, watching me. "You would be much prettier if your hair was flowing down your shoulders," he says. "You should exercise your chest muscles to puff up your breasts since you are almost grown up."

I am surprised he is talking to me like that, and for a moment I feel grown up and important. This man is older and maybe smarter than me and is suggesting things that will help me grow up faster. The man has very dark eyes, but he smiles a lot. He starts asking me exactly where I live and who lives in my house and who is home right now. I don't think much about the danger and tell him that I will be home by myself. When he asks me why I am going home in the middle of the day, I tell him I have a headache and I need to go home to lie down. He tells me to rest a while under the big tree.

Once I have cooled my feet in the creek and had a drink, I am eager to get to town as quickly as possible. My headache and nausea have not gone away, and the ride might get me home faster. "Even though he is ugly and smelly," I think, "he has actually been very kind to me. After all, he stopped for my and the horse's benefit. I don't see any harm in continuing with him to Topola. Maybe I will rest for just a few minutes first."

But as I am resting on the dried grass, I start thinking about what I said to him, how I blabbered to him about me being all grown up and how I will be home all by myself. I get scared, thinking that he might come into my house and kill me or do something worse, and I start to cry.

I quickly get up, and with a sudden piercing pang in my stomach I realize that I am missing my parents dreadfully. I tell him, "I have changed my mind about going home to Topola. I want to go back to the farm where my parents are." I start to run back toward where my parents are. Those four kilometers seem so far away, and it seems so long ago since I left them this morning.

Behind me, I hear the man jump down from the wagon. When I glance back over my shoulder, he is running after me with his belly flopping and his few strands of hair blowing around in the air behind him. He is catching up. I am scared of what he might do to me if he catches me. It sounds like he is right behind me. Then I trip, and he falls on top of me.

Trapped under this big mountain of a man, I feel like gagging. He smells like he hasn't washed for days. I am panicking and trying to yell but no sound comes out of my mouth. I am thinking, "I am going to die." After he wriggles his body off me, he tries to calm me down, insisting that he only has my best interest in mind.

"Get back in the wagon or you will roast in this heat walking back to see your parents." I plead and cry, but he ignores me, pushing me toward the wagon and tugging at my pigtails.

This time he sits me right beside him, up on the small wooden bench, and he keeps his right hand on my left thigh as we navigate down the potholed road toward town. I close my eyes and force myself to dream of how I will be on the train out of Topola today.

Chapter Two

☙ ❧

As I open my eyes, I can see in the distance my uncle's farm house. I am praying under my breath that one of my relatives will be outside doing some chores and will see us.

The wagon driver tells me he now knows where I live, and if I do anything stupid, he will find me again. "Keep your mouth shut," he says. "I will do the talking."

We approach Uncle Barnabek's farm, which is just a smidge off the road, and I see my uncle outside, working in his yard. I am very excited that finally someone will rescue me from God knows what, but I stay silent. My uncle waves to us and yells "hello," but he keeps working. I can see that the driver is only slowing down a little; he is not going to stop. I hold my tummy, and bend forward like I am going to throw up. Walking toward the wagon, my uncle asks me, "Who are you with, Krysia? Is everything okay?"

The wagon driver introduces himself. "Hello, I am Ed. I was visiting relatives from a bordering village," he explains. "I brought them some meat and now I am driving home from

Szczekazow through Topola. Krysia was walking home because she is sick, and I am giving her a ride."

"That is very nice of you to do that, Ed," my uncle says, and he waves to us and goes back to his chores.

I don't know what to do. Maybe Ed is just a nice guy who is trying to help me, and I have been letting my imagination run wild. Maybe everything will be alright. But I am praying again.

I live at the far end of the community, so we will have to travel through the whole town. But as we approach Topola, Ed decides to use the back road. Wagons do not usually travel on that road because of the steep hill, and it is even rougher than the main road. "It is the shortcut to your place," he tells me. "And there are hardly any people on the road, so we can get to your house much faster." This does not seem right to me. The road should not be busy, because everyone is at their farm.

No one will be at home, either. My grandparents, who live in the other half of our house, are on their piece of land two kilometers the other side of town, and they will not be home until suppertime. Our neighbors next door on both sides are also on their farms for the day, just like everyone else. I close my eyes and pray, "God, give me inspiration to find a plan. And please do it very quickly."

We lurch through a large pothole, and I open my eyes. We are about three doors away from my house. Old Mrs. Bujacka is sitting outside on her steps, so I say, "There is Grandma. She will look after me, and you don't have to worry about me anymore. Grandma, I am home!"

Ed looks like he does not believe what I am saying. Mrs. Bujacka does not move. "Grandma," I call, "it is me, Krysia!"

When Ed slows down his horse for a large pothole, I jump off the wagon and run and hug Mrs. Bujacka. She has 12 grandchildren, 11 great-grandchildren and who knows how many great-great-grandchildren. She is very old and partially deaf and mostly blind, so she sometimes gets to stay home and look after the house and prepare supper for everyone who is working on the farm.

Mrs. Bujacka looks a little confused, but she lets me hug her and she doesn't say a word. She probably thinks I am one of her relatives from out of town who she doesn't get to see too often.

Ed gets out of the wagon to say hello, but the old woman doesn't acknowledge him. I hug her again and ask, "What's for dinner, Grandma?"

She smiles and says, "Potatoes, what else."

Ed's eyes narrow, and he stares at us. Then he fixes something on the horse's mouth and gets on the wagon, saying, "Remember what I told you earlier, just be a good girl." Finally, he drives off.

I stand beside the old woman, still trembling with fear. Have I fooled him? Maybe. But maybe he knows I live three doors over.

A shiver goes down my spine. What if he comes back and hurts Mrs. Bujacka or both of us? After pacing back and forth in front of Mrs. Bujacka for what seems like an hour, I decide to walk to my house. I check our front yard and then our back yard to make sure Ed is not here. I keep thinking that by now he must have figured out I live here instead of with that nice old lady.

There is no sign of him, or any other person—just some chickens, ducks, and geese running around, and the rooster coming to greet me. Our dog has a long chain from the barn all the way to the house, and he makes an extra noise when he sees me.

I feel protected for now, at least. Finding the house key in the hiding spot, I open the door and say, "Hello house, I am finally home." I heave a sigh of relief. Then I start to get an eerie feeling of being all alone. I have been here without adults many times before and have always been fine. Mostly I was babysitting my infant brothers, but this time it is different.

"I will be alright, I will be alright," I keep repeating to myself. Our dog barks, and I hear a voice. Is it Ed? I start praying, "God save me, I have much to do." Looking out through our window, I see the neighbor that lives behind us talking to our dog and patting his head before he crosses through our yard.

People have cut through our property for as long as I can remember. Sometimes it is scary for us, especially when we are all alone. We mostly see kids after school, and an occasional stranger, and we never know who will be crossing next.

Maybe Ed will come back. I feel more and more frightened, and I need somewhere to hide. Locking our door behind me, I hurry around to the other side of the house, to where Grandma Kula has a cellar.

Years ago, our house was one big room and my father's parents lived with us. But Grandma was always telling Mom she shouldn't be sick all the time instead of working on the farm. Mom always complained to Dad about Grandma's disapproval of her. And Mom also complained about Dad doing what Grandma thought he should do. "Why are you listening to your mother all the time," she would ask, "instead of taking care of your family your own way?" Then they would start fighting with each other.

This went on for many years, until one day Dad had enough and told Grandma, "I am going to build a wall between us. This house will be divided in half. And from now on I will be making my own decisions."

I don't know what Grandpa Kula thought, but he was probably glad the fighting was mostly over, too.

The cellar ended up on Grandma and Grandpa's side of the house. As I quietly close the trap door above my head and carefully feel my way down the short ladder, I am shaking. "No one will find me here," I reassure myself, but I don't know which is worse, this dark hole or the wagon driver's threat to come after me.

I continue with my prayers as I fumble around in the dark. Bumping into a long shelf full of last year's canned cherries and plums, I remember that Grandma has a small stool in the far corner. Feeling my way toward it, I step on something that is moving.

What was that?

It was probably only a mouse, I tell myself.

But what if it wasn't?

My heart is beating rapidly. And now I don't care if Ed is outside waiting for me—I cannot stay in that dark cellar one more minute. Besides, if I pack quickly, I can get to the train station and be safe from him. So I scramble to the top of the stairs and run outside, still praying for God to save me.

On my way back to our side of the house, the barn reminds me of why I need to leave this town. Judgmental people. Gossips. What do they know anyway? I must get away from Topola.

It seemed impossible, and now I have my miracle. The money my dad gave me to pay the bill at the corner store is in my pocket, along with the few coins I had been able to save. I tell myself my prayers have been answered.

God will keep me safe. I only need to pack, and then I can go.

Chapter Three

My few belongings are in the suitcase, and I reach down and snap it closed. I am ready to go to the train station, with time to spare. Ed has not returned, and the dog is quiet in the yard. I have finally calmed down enough to stop and take one long last look around the tiny building that has been my home for my whole life.

We live on the edge of town in a small one-room house built out of cement blocks. The old cookstove on the left side of the room burns coal, wood, cow patties and anything else we can find on the farm. The stove has a rusted top with many scrapes and scratches on the steel cover, showing it has been well used. It has four burners and a flap to stoke the fire. A pail full of water sits beside it at all times. The chimney, a big round pipe from the back of the stove, goes all the way through our ceiling.

The two-foot-long shelf above the stove has our dishes on it to keep them warm. On the wall behind the stove, pots and pans hang from nails. All four walls are wooden planks, unpainted and about six inches wide. A small statue of baby Jesus and the Virgin Mary is on the shelf above the dishes. The only decorations on the wall are a picture of the Virgin Mary holding baby Jesus, and two crosses with Jesus on them.

The white basin for washing and bathing sits on a small four-legged table in the corner behind the stove. Water seems to be in it at all times. We all use it to wash up when we come from outside, and Mom is always washing her hands between chores. A small dark green towel hangs on the left side of the wash table on a big hook. Below, under the table, sits the slop pail to throw away the dirty water. Beside the small table sits another pail with clean drinking water and it is covered tightly.

In the middle of the room is the potbelly stove, which keeps us warm in the winter months. A large pipe is attached to the back of this stove and goes right through the ceiling to the outside. Occasionally, we must light it for a quick drying of our clothes and diapers.

We have a four-legged wooden table that sits by the window, with four mismatched chairs. On the right side of the room along the wall are two single beds, heads butted together. One bed is for Mom and Dad and the other was for me and my two younger brothers until the day, while Mom was in the hospital, I complained to Dad that I needed my own bed. He gave me a choice. "You can sleep on the floor or in the barn, it is up to you." Grandma came over and gave me an old blanket, and I used it to make a bed behind our tall dresser. That dresser is our last item of furniture. It has two front mirror doors, and it holds the clothing for the five of us.

There is no television in our house, but we do have a small radio. It only works once in a while and we are not allowed to touch it. Dad uses the radio for occasional news about politics.

Many times, beginning when I was only five years old, I have been confined in this small space for the entire day. It was up to me to feed my little brothers and keep them occupied while Dad was working on the farm and Mom was away at the hospital.

Closing the door behind me, I lock it and put the key back in its hiding place. Our house is situated a long ways from the main road, on a long narrow plot of land that backs onto the road behind us. On the right side of the house is a driveway, deeply grooved from our wagon driving in the wet mud. Plum and apple trees line the driveway and soften the harsh look of the rutted path.

The front of the house has no windows and the ground slopes uphill to our well, which is surrounded by chamomile. At the back of the house is a patch of tall flowers reaching almost to our windows. My favorite is the morning glory. I can smell the flowers all over our back yard, which is a sanctuary for all our small animals.

A few feet away is a deep hole, where we toss the manure from the animals. We use it to fertilize our land and our flowers. The outhouse is right next to the animal barn, and next to that is the big barn for storing hay and wheat. It has large front doors which open right through to the back and onto our large vegetable garden. I don't want to think about the barn right now, or about what happened there.

Next is Dad's workshop with many tools and old wagon parts. He is always fixing something in there and we are not allowed inside. Back toward the house, on the left side, is a large cherry tree. It provides much enjoyment and we have had many good feedings from that tree. We have one cellar under Grandma and Grandpa's side of the house for fruit and preserves, and another two outside for our root vegetables.

Fall is always a very busy time, when we gather the root vegetables and grain for the winter. The grain has to be beaten out of the straw and taken to the mill for our flour. I get to help out with this ritual of beating it for hours and gathering grain into the sacks. We tie the straw up into big bundles and use it for our animal beds. After the straw is used as bedding it is combined with the manure to make compost. Cleaning the barn is my least favorite job, but we all take turns helping Dad. Taking the manure outside and dumping it in an open pit in our back yard is just about the ultimate for the smell. Most days if the wind blows just right, it will carry the smell of manure right into the house.

The sun is warm on my head, and the changing shadows in the yard snap me out of my daydreaming. I hurry to the train station, so I won't miss the next train.

At the station, a few people have gathered on the platform. So far, there is no one I know. I stand at the edge of the tracks with wonder, trying to imagine what is beyond this place. A dim light appears in the distance: the train is coming. It looks like it is standing still for a moment, not moving at all. Then I feel trembling beneath my feet, as the whistle splits the air and the train's stack blows dirty gray smoke. Now it is drawing quickly up to the station, a shuddering steel animal that trembles and snorts under the beautiful blue sky.

My heart pounds with anticipation. Metal screeching on metal makes a horrible sound as the brakes go on. I cover my ears as the front of the train passes me, and people hurry toward the passenger doors as it comes to a halt. I move forward with them, watching the faces of all the people dismounting from the train, and my stomach is beginning to sink. What is my dad going to say when he finds out I am gone? Should I really go through with this? Will I get into trouble for using my parents' food money?

What about my mom? I always help her with cooking, peeling vegetables, getting water from the well, doing dishes, milking the cow, feeding animals, cleaning the house and all those other small jobs. She will have to do everything now, and she always looks so exhausted.

I look like my mom, except she has dark brown hair, much darker than mine. She has lines around her eyes, but not from laughing. She cries all the time. Who will help her when I am not there? How can I leave her to do all the work? Sure, she has Dad and my two young brothers, but they don't help much, especially around the house.

But this is the chance I have been praying for. I say to myself, "I am never coming back to this place as long as I live." Then something tugs at my heart strings and I feel really badly for thinking like this and for leaving.

The city of Sosnoviec is in the middle of Poland. Will I be safe by myself? The train is huge. I look at the conductor's black suit, and panic sets in. I feel a spasm in my chest as I move forward with the crowd. The steel steps are very steep and a nice man gives me a hand to climb up with my suitcase. "Here you go child, be careful."

On the top step I quickly turn around as if to wave to a loved one, but there is no one to see me off. Turning, I pray instead. "Lord, come with me on this journey as it is unknown to me. Hold me tight and keep me safe."

The conductor shows me to a seat and says, "I will put your suitcase up above your head on the luggage carrier."

"No, thank you," I insist. "I will need things from my suitcase during the trip and I wouldn't be able to reach way up there."

"Keep it close to you on the floor," he says with a wink. "Be good. I will see you later."

As the train pulls away from the station, I look out of the window across the open land as it moves away from me. I think back to when I was five years old and to all the days that made me decide to leave Topola and our farm behind.

PART II

❧ 1955 to 1960 ❦

Chapter Four

❧ ❦

It is hot in the kitchen because the wood stove seems to always be fired up even though it is summer. Heavy rain is
coming down, filling up our outside barrel with extra water.
Rain makes a big mess. But at five, I like to play with my little
brother in the backyard mudhole.

The horse is standing by the barn with his head down and is
getting wet. I don't think he likes the rain. Fog and mist are ris-
ing off of the back road and I can hardly see the white stone
statue of the Virgin Mary. She sits by the road, surrounded by a
small fence, two houses over from us.

Every May, the people of our neighborhood gather here to
worship Mary. During the warm evenings, candles burn around
the statue. We sing praises to her and ask her for our daily
support.

Dad is back and he is not alone. Dr. Wacilek with his little
black bag and smiley teeth says, "Hello." He is here to examine
Mom. He looks very worried. "She has to leave now," he tells
my dad. "She has lost a lot of blood."

As Mom says goodbye, I hang on to her hand until it slips away. Her words echo through my head. "In case I don't come back, look after your brothers."

I cry and sob and I don't want her to go, but she must get to the hospital quickly. The doctor is telling her, "Hurry up and get going as the journey to the hospital is long. I want you to make it this time before it is too late."

I run through the rain to Grandma Kula's side of the house, hoping she will know what to do.

Grandma is a very serious, determined, and fussy lady. She loves to cook and bake, and she loves to eat a lot. She puts pepper on everything she eats, so much that she can't see what she is eating. My eyes water when I come over to see her at dinnertime. The smell of pepper will linger through the house all night.

She sometimes shows me how to bake her favorite cakes and then we taste them afterward. She does little things for me constantly and encourages me no matter what I complain about. I have protection in Grandma's arms from my parents as well. When they are arguing, I escape outside and sneak to her side of the house. She always calms me down and makes things better.

Grandma's face is always very serious. She is much bigger than my mom. Her gray hair is long and it is always pulled back into a bun. She wears a long black skirt to the ground and a multi-color blouse with different colored little flowers around the collar. She wears flat shoes because her feet swell up at night. She has a heart condition and takes drops that Grandpa makes for her. I hope she will live a long life because I need her.

Grandpa and my dad are scared of Grandma. Whatever she says, that's what they do.

I am not sure why Grandma likes me. I question everything I see and hear, and Grandma tells me, "You are my smart girl," and that makes me feel good. She buys me pretty hair ribbons and weaves them into my braids, and she tells me I look all grown up. Grandma hugs me often, and she tells me, "With your mind always engaged, one day you will be very important and help others." I smile and close my eyes to see the picture she describes to me until she says sternly, "Now enough daydreaming; get back to work if you want any of this to ever happen for you."

Grandma gives my dad orders all the time. Dad is married and has a family, but she doesn't think he can do a good job. She tells Dad, "Plow my acres first, and then do yours later." He has to fertilize, pull weeds, and harvest her land first, before he gets to ours.

Grandma controls Dad and all of his decisions about how he should be running our farm. Dad sometimes gets angry with her. Then he storms out very frustrated and he takes it out on Mom.

Grandma also tells Mom, "You are not good enough for my son and you never should have got married in the first place." Since Dad separated Grandma's side of the house from ours, she cries a lot because of the wall, so I go sit on her knee and comfort her and she asks, "Will you still come over to visit me often? I couldn't stand it if I lost you as well."

I assure her, "I will see you as much as I did before," but deep inside I know things will change.

The vegetable garden behind the barn is Grandma's, but we used to be able to grow our food in one corner. Now that the wall is up, things are very tense around here. My parents hardly speak with Grandma, and she uses me as a go-between. She tells me things like, "Deliver a message to your mom that the garden belongs to Grandma and your parents are not allowed to use it."

"We have to go eight kilometers to get our daily food," I say to Grandma, but she says nothing to that.

Grandma swears at Mom when our stove gets lit, as the smoke fills Grandma's side. When Grandma lights the stove on her side, our side fills with smoke as well. She tells me, "Your mother doesn't know how to light the stove, cook, or anything else."

After months of them bickering about the smoke, a neighbor showed Grandma how to fix this problem. Grandma didn't understand that we had only one vent for the whole house and it was located on her side, and it had nothing to do with Mom. But she still blames Mom for everything and she is very mean to Mom and always calls her bad names to us kids. She often swears at Mom for stealing her son as well.

Grandma hates Mom for telling Dad about her behavior toward Mom, and she also blames Mom for the house separation. She tells me, "It is your mother's fault that we are not together. She causes so much grief for all of us, we would be better off without her."

I am filled with discontent. It is mostly true what Grandma is saying about Mom. She seems to be continually fighting with Dad about something, and I cannot talk with her like I can with Grandma. She doesn't really hear me. She prays a lot and mutters to herself, "Why did I get talked into this marriage? I should have gone to be a nun like I wanted to."

But now Mommy is gone.

అ ళ

When I wake up the next morning, the rain has stopped and the sun is shining again. I ask Daddy when Mommy will come back. He says not for a few days. I ask if she is sick again, and he tells me she is having a baby.

Now that Mommy is gone, Daddy is not sure what to do with us. I am five years old, my brother Stan is three, and my brother Jim is only one. Grandma and Grandpa have already gone to work their field for the day. So have all the other adults and they have taken their children with them. Older children must either go to school or help work the land, every day, unless it is raining too hard. But Dad will not be able to get anything done if he takes us with him, and we are too small to help.

After we have finished the morning chores, Dad sits us down and tells us, "Be good kids and find something to do while I am gone. I will be back at suppertime." He takes a half loaf of bread and a jar of cold water and goes outside to hitch our horse to the wagon. He will drive the eight kilometers to our land to do the work he must do to provide for us. He has no choice but to lock us up and leave us all alone. This is what must be done for the family to survive, and so he does it.

He gives us the key just in case of any emergency, so we can get out. "If there is a problem, watch for someone you know using the shortcut through our yard. Schoolchildren, or our neighbors. You can pass them the key and they will let you out. But don't let strangers see you." He kneels down to look me in the eyes. "Strangers might be gypsies. They go through our town and steal eggs and chickens. And they can steal you. Never let strangers see that you are home alone."

Dad hugs us, then looks at me again. "Be a good girl and look after your brothers." After one last hug, he closes the door and we hear the padlock snap shut. He walks toward the wagon without turning around or waving to us.

It must break his heart to leave us all alone.

As we watch Dad drive away, a sinking feeling comes over me. What am I going to do with my two baby brothers all day? What am I going to feed them? How can we keep busy all day and be good? What if the gypsies come?

I lay on the bed with my face pressed into the pillow and cry until my eyes are too sore to see. After a while, my three-year-old brother comes over to me and pats me on the back. "Don't cry," Stan tells me. "I will be good today."

When I look into his sad eyes, I know I need to be strong for the boys as well as for me. I give baby Jim a bottle of milk and put him in his crib. He falls asleep quickly. Stan and I decide to draw pictures of things we see around us and color them with bright pencils. We make faces at ourselves in the double mirror on our clothes dresser, the only mirror we have.

I make Grandma's famous raspberry jelly sandwiches for lunch. We have lots of raspberries growing behind the barn. Grandma makes jelly every year and stores it in the cellar under her floor.

A whining noise is coming from the rocking crib. Jim is waking up. He is fussing a lot, so I pour him another bottle of milk, but this time he doesn't want it and starts crying louder.

Changing Jim's diaper is challenging, as he is kicking and screaming at the top of his lungs. After this loud performance, he falls asleep. I don't want to waste water washing the diaper, so I leave it in a small bucket to soak. I cannot get another bucket of water from our well behind the house until Dad gets home.

Stan is very restless, and I keep promising him candies if he will continue to color with me. I don't have any money to buy candies, but my promises keep him quiet and he does listen to me for short periods of time.

I pour him some milk and am trying to fill Jim's bottle when Stan jumps up and knocks the milk on the floor. I scream, "You stupid boy, now what are we going to do?"

We need milk for baby Jim and for us, for the rest of the day. What are we going to drink? We will have to wait until we hear someone outside and then, if it is someone we know, we can attract attention.

After a while, we see our neighbor, Janek, crossing our yard. We bang on our windows calling, "Please let us out, please let us out," until he comes to see us. I shout, "We need to get some milk for our baby. Our milk got spilled on the floor and we don't have any left." I ask him to open the door, and I slip the key through the space underneath.

After a while, Janek opens the door and says, "Be careful with the young ones."

I carry Jim, and Stan and I run to the corner store a few blocks down the road to get some milk on credit. The trip isn't easy but we make it, and now we have enough milk to last until supper.

Chapter Five

It has been many days, and still Mom has not come home. We are locked in the house again. The afternoon sun is coming around our back yard when I see two boys from town using the shortcut. Stan and I bang on the windows to get their attention, and they come over to see us.

The older boy says, "Where are your parents?"

"Dad is at the farm," I answer, "and Mom is in the hospital in the big city."

"Have you been in the house all day?"

I nod.

He is looking at the padlock on the door. "Do you want to come out and play for a while?"

We pass them the key, and we are free in an instant. Stan goes out of the house like a shot and starts running around the yard chasing our chickens. He doesn't listen to me once we are outside. I drag Jimmy out of the crib and put him on the ground under the cherry tree. The two neighborhood boys and I climb the tree to get some cherries.

Stan is nowhere to be found, but I am not worried because he always runs around the yard and hides, even when Dad is working in the yard. I know he is not too far from us.

Jimmy starts to crawl around the tree and is eating cherries that fall on the ground. He is happy for the time being. I have big pockets in my petticoat in which to put my cherries. The two neighborhood boys are much higher on the tree where the cherries are bigger and sweeter. The sun is shining all around us and I feel alive. As I soak up the sun, I feel very grateful that these boys let us out.

My daydreaming comes to a halt when I notice my dad coming up the driveway early.

I don't remember much after that, except for him yelling and screaming at us. "How can you be so ungrateful and do such a dangerous thing?"

I see Jim's face is all red from eating cherries, and I'm not sure how many pits he has swallowed. I hope he won't have a tummy ache tomorrow. "He could have choked to death and you didn't care about that," Dad is yelling at me. "Look at him, he is dirty and his face is all red."

He sees Stan on the roof of the barn and yells to him, "Come down this instant." He takes his belt off and lays Stan on the bench on the front porch and spanks him hard. Then he turns to me. "Now, take Jimmy in the house and clean him up, and I will deal with you later."

I hurry into the house and clean up baby Jim. The water is red, so I pour it into the diaper pail. The cloth diapers are now pink and I pray they will come out white when I wash them tomorrow.

Quickly I start to peel potatoes. We have a very quiet supper of boiled potatoes with sour milk, and then we all get ready for bed.

Dad is very angry and tells me, "The trust is broken between us and I can't take any chances of leaving you like this again." I have no idea what he has in store for us tomorrow when he leaves for work. I hope maybe we will be able to go with him, but I don't think so.

I will try not to worry about that tonight. I pretend I am all grown up and keep praying.

∾ ∾

In the morning I am already looking forward to a brand-new day. Feeding chickens and ducks is fun, as they all chase me to get food.

Daddy is ready to leave us again, but this time is different. He is looking for his hammer and large nails. "Damn, where are they?" He looks at Stan, who plays with everything he sees. "What have you done with my stuff?"

Stan points outside to Dad's tool box which he'd dragged out from the shed the other day and left under the cherry tree. Dad is already upset and irritated and I am afraid of what he will do with his tools.

He says goodbye to us and tells us to be good for the day. He locks the door from the outside as usual, except this time he doesn't give us the key. Instead, he pounds long nails around the windows and the door and twists them into the frames so no one will attempt to open them while he is gone for the day.

Stan and I watch with our faces glued to the windows and tears running down our cheeks. I am screaming and banging on the window as hard as I can, but Dad never turns back to look at us. He jumps on the wagon and leaves for the day.

I'm trapped in a one-room house with my two baby brothers again, and this time we are really trapped. Dad is doing this for our own safety, so he says, but it feels like a prison to me.

I cry and cry until my eyes are swollen. Then I look at my little brothers' sad faces, and I have to stop feeling anything but survival. I have to be strong for them. There is no one we can talk to or count on to help us.

What about if something happens to baby Jim? He is so little and helpless. I change his diaper and put the soggy one to soak in the big pail with soapy water, with the diapers from the day before. I'm getting Jim's bottle ready when Stan starts pulling on my dress, and I spill warm milk all over the baby.

"Stan!" I yell. "You stupid, bad boy, you always want attention. You are going to get it when Dad gets home."

"I don't care," he says. But he goes to the table to color some pictures.

When I'm done with Jim, I join Stan at the table. We are still drawing quietly when we see two faces glued to the window. They are staring at us.

"Quick, Stan," I say. "Jump off the chair and we will hide under the table so no one can see us." Before too long, Stan wants to go and see who is outside. But then he sees that I am crying in fear, and he starts to cry, too. After I calm him down, I look to see if the faces are gone. They are, and we come out from under the table and go back to our drawings.

Later in the morning, I see a shadow. Someone is moving in our yard. Stan and I go to the window and peek out carefully. A man is standing by the barn. It is our neighbor Wojtek, and he is borrowing my Dad's sickle for cutting his grain. Now our faces are glued to the window. He notices us as he is crossing our yard, and he comes toward the house. We duck under the table and stay still until he leaves. It is a scary day today and I am desperately waiting for Dad to return home.

After lunch, I change baby Jim into his last outfit, and I decide to warm up the pail of water that sits on the stove at all times. Matches are handy, and a small stack of kindling is beside the stove. It is ready to start the fire for cooking our dinner when Dad gets home at night.

I pull the chair against the stove while it is warming the wash water. I pour some soap into the water, maybe a little too much. The bubbles are coming out of the pail and onto the stove and spilling on the dirt floor. The smell of burning soap is much worse than Jim's dirty diapers.

The kindling wood lasts long enough to warm the water but it finally dies down. Now both boys are screaming very loud. Jim is howling like someone is beating him up, and Stan is yelling, "I will tell Dad that you tried to burn our house down."

I tell him that he will be taken away from us for being bad all the time.

The clean-up is long and exhausting. The lingering smell of burned soap and sticky residue on the stove makes Dad ask lots of questions. "What happened here today?" Stan is being quiet for a change while I do all the explaining and minimize the soap accident. Clothes and diapers are hanging around the room to dry most of the time. I am thankful that Dad doesn't notice my new batch of laundry or ask any more questions about my washing, he just shakes his head.

After a supper of boiled potatoes with butter and a glass of milk, I am scrubbing the stove again so Dad won't figure out what happened earlier. Then I put the boys to bed.

Finally both boys fall asleep.

Most evenings, Dad and I sit and discuss his day. He tells me, "The wheat fields are getting on well this year and we should have a good crop in the fall. We need more rain so the weeds will be easier to pull. The pig is getting fat, and we should be good for a few months with some new smoked meat."

Sometimes he tells me about our animals. Dad believes he has some kind of gift for talking to our animals. "Our horse listens to me and pulls the wagon along the rough road with deep holes. I look right into his eyes and tell him he can do it. The horse nods and gives me his okay, and does what I ask him to do."

Sometimes he whispers into their ears. Our milk cow, Babunia, is very precious. She produces lots of milk to feed our family and our grandparents and the left over is for our pigs. During the hot weather, Dad prays for rain so the long grass will keep Babunia cooler. "Cows are the gentlest breathing creatures," Dad tells me, "and none of the animals show more passionate tenderness to their young when they are deprived of them." When the time comes to kill one of our animals to eat, Dad doesn't want to do it. "That is your mom's job," he says.

But tonight, Dad has fallen asleep across his bed with his boots still on. After I remove them I cover him up, say my prayers, and blow out our oil lamp. I lie in bed for a long while, thinking about Mom and Dad, and how hard they work. I think of how Mom is sick a lot and stays away from us most of the time to get better. I wonder if she misses her parents. They moved far away to Canada before I was born.

There must be more out there to this life than I know so far. I pray that one day soon God will bring my mom home healthy and some good will come to us.

I don't want to think about tomorrow, when we will be captive in our home again with nails on our door and windows.

Chapter Six

࿊ ࿋

Today we are having a quiet day. Stan is counting lumps of coal on the floor, Jim is sleeping, and I am drawing birds at the kitchen table. Suddenly our dog, Teddy, starts barking, and we hear people talking outside. I peek out the window to see what is going on.

A tall man holding a dark bird is coming toward our front door. I step back from the window and cover Jim's head with a blanket so whoever is out there will not see him sleeping. Then I grab Stan's hand, and we hide under the table. The man is banging on the door and Teddy is barking furiously. I hear our chickens scattering around and making noises. More voices, a man and a woman, shouting. Are the gypsies here? I pray baby Jim will stay asleep, and that he will not suffocate under the blanket.

After what seems like hours, the noise finally stops. Slowly we stand up and peek outside. No one is there.

Now the sinking feeling of being alone with two babies while strangers come into our yard is overwhelming. I don't want to think about the fact that they might hurt us or kidnap us. We try not to make too much noise, but it isn't easy to be quiet with a crying baby and an active three-year-old who wants to climb the walls and everything else in his sight. At least now he is busy with the coal, making a big mess everywhere.

We hear outside noises once again and the knocking is louder the second time around. Stan is going toward the door, and I have to stop him and cover his mouth so he won't talk and let the strangers know we are home alone. I whisper in his ear, promising him candies if he comes back under the table and is quiet for a little while. I have forgotten to cover Jim. "Please don't let them look in the window and see him," I pray.

My hand is bleeding, and I realize Stan bit my hand. I must have been holding him too tight. How long was I covering his mouth?

Finally Teddy stops barking. I peek through the curtains and it is quiet outside. No one is in the yard anymore. The dog's rope is tangled up from jumping so much. He has been very upset, but no one can help him. Then a couple of chickens appear; the thieves didn't get them all.

Our bird clock is chiming ten, and I realize we still have a whole day ahead of us. Dad won't be home until dark, and neither will Grandma and Grandpa.

I wrap a tea towel around my bleeding hand and pretend nothing just happened outside. Stan constantly asks, "Who was that?" I start singing, and I pick up the coals off our floor and put them into our potbelly stove. Stan is dirty from playing with the coal, so I wash him. It feels like I have been scrubbing him for about an hour and he is still dirty. It is time to make some jelly sandwiches and milk for lunch, before baby Jim wakes up.

After lunch I put Jim to bed, and then I hear more noise outside. Our dog is eating something by the barn. I see a man dressed in black and wearing a funny-looking hat. He is grabbing our chickens and ducks. A small boy is helping him to chase them around.

This time I drag Stan behind the tall dresser, promising him candies if he will be quiet. Then the noise stops again. If they have caught the last of our chickens and ducks, we can breathe for a while. They won't be back to our place until another day, I hope.

When Dad comes home he is worried. "A gypsy caravan was parked at the other side of town," he says. "I saw it when I was coming home."

He tells us more about the gypsies. People are afraid of them. They have been showing up in their covered wagons, telling our townsfolk that they are travelling Christians. They wander from house to house, asking for animals, eggs, vegetables and any other food people can spare, and some people will give them their last loaf of bread for fear of something worse happening. When they know that everyone is away on their piece of land and no one is home during the day, they steal chickens, ducks, eggs and anything else they can put in their wagons. When people are home, they have a way of mesmerizing them with their fortune-telling, while another member of their group sneaks around and steals something.

"The gypsies are handy in many things," Dad says. "They have time on their hands to learn different skills. They have no home and no land, only their wagons, and every day they move to a different town. Don't ever open the door for them or speak with them, as they would steal you also, and use you to steal for them in the next town."

Dad goes to check on the animals, and when he returns he is some upset. "We have lost all the eggs, some of the chickens and a duck. And I found trampled flowers under all the windows, which shows they were looking in."

Maybe it is a good thing our windows were nailed shut.

Later, when our grandparents get home, Grandpa tells us more stories about gypsies, about their long coats, their tall hats and how they hide stolen things in them, and how sneaky they are. We must always be on guard when they come around to our place, especially when we are alone.

❧ ❧

Dad and his wagon are long gone to the farm, and Mom is still in the hospital, so I am trying to think what to cook for us three kids. How do I keep my brothers busy today?

"Today, we will make pasta just like Mom makes it," I announce, dragging the bread board onto the table. Stan looks doubtful, but I say, "I have seen Mom make pasta a few times, and I know what she puts in it." I bring out milk, flour and eggs, but I don't remember in what order to put them on the board.

Stan passes me four eggs and I crack them on the board, then pour milk on them. As they run off the board, all over the table, and onto the floor, I quickly try to stop them by sprinkling on some flour. Now the flour, the eggs and the milk are all over the dirt floor.

Stan's yelling wakes up the baby, and Jim starts crying. The mess from eggs, milk and flour is everywhere. Kneeling on the floor, trying to clean up the muddy mess, I am overwhelmed. I cover my eyes and cry.

After a while, I feel a gentle little hand on my cheek. "Don't cry, Krysia," says Stan. "I will help you clean up." At three years old, Stan is a handful and some days he is uncontrollable, but today I see a different brother with gentle helping hands.

It takes hours, but we finally finish before Dad comes home. I cook some potatoes and serve them with sour milk and we all go to bed, exhausted.

Morning comes early, and Dad is getting ready to go to the farm. I hear birds chirping outside our window, chickens and roosters making morning noises, and our goat giving his okay that morning is here again.

After our chores of feeding chickens and pigs, Dad leaves us once again to fend for ourselves for the day. For lunch, I find a jar of Grandma's canned cherries and a bucket of carrots that Dad got out of the root cellar last night. He always milks the cow before he leaves, so we have enough milk for today.

"After lunch when the cleanup is over, we will play a game," I say. "We will prick some potatoes on our forks and pretend they are soldiers coming to rescue us."

With Mom away in the hospital and Dad always on the farm, we have no money for any extra food or toys, so we play with whatever things we have. Occasionally we play with spoons. "No knives," Dad said last week, since Stan has cut himself a couple of times already.

Our forks are soon talking to each other and the time passes by. Next, we stand in front of the only mirror in our house. It has been a constant source of entertainment for us. Before Mom left to go to the hospital, Dad got drunk with his friends and pushed Mom against the dresser and the mirror cracked in two places.

The mirror is still secured in the wardrobe. But our images now are different. It seems like there are an extra two images of each of us to play with. We count how many faces we can make and laugh at who can make a better face.

Stan gets restless and loses interest quickly. He spills milk all over himself and on Jimmy, and once again our cleanup begins. When we come back to the mirror, we take our clothes off and observe how we look in the mirror. Stan flexes his muscles, smiles and states, "I am the king . . . Wrahhhhh!"

Chapter Seven

❦

Another new day, and the sun is showing up around the barn. Our animals are running around waiting to get fed. After the frenzy with feeding is over, all the animals are happy and settle down.

Dad adjusts the horse's muzzle as he prepares to leave to the farm again. "Be good today," were his last words as he nailed the house shut. Now he waves his usual goodbye, and I stare out the window watching his wagon leaving our driveway. The overwhelming feeling of loneliness is upon me. When is Mommy coming home? Why doesn't Dad take us with him?

I know that what he always says is true. "I get a lot more done when I don't have to worry about you guys running around all over the fields and getting hurt." And there is a baby to think about; what would Dad do with Jimmy? Working all day in the baking sun and worrying about feeding us kids and our safety is just too much for him. And Grandma and Grandpa agree with him. This is just the way things have to be, until Mom comes home.

But I still feel lost and abandoned.

After staring out the window for a long while, I turn around to see two small faces looking at me, just as lost as I am, and I know I have to act capable of staying home and looking after things. Today is going to be a great day. We will sing and play and draw pictures and I won't be sad any longer.

For the best part of the early morning, I keep my brothers busy. We play games of hide-and-go-seek under towels on our heads, laughing often. After feeding and changing baby Jim, I put him down to have a nap. Jim enjoys his warm milk, and after sucking on the bottle he is very tired and falls asleep. In the quiet moments, Stan and I do some drawing.

After lunch I put Jim into the cradle that Dad made for me a few years ago, when I was a baby. The cradle is almost to my chest, and at five years old I think I am quite tall. There are wooden bars on the front and back, about four inches apart, with rounded edges. The two sides each have a solid wall with a curve on the top, and there is a small design of two leaves together on the left wall. The legs connect to a curved shape in front and back, for better cradling, my dad says. The bottom of the bed is wooden and covered with many blankets.

The cradle is light brown in color and very shiny, as Mom is always wiping it. She says, "Babies always put everything in their mouth and Jim loves to chew on the edges, so it needs to be clean."

With two rockers on each end, the cradle is easy to rock back and forth. Mom likes to rock it with her foot while she is doing something else. Until now, I had never sat on the cradle to rock Jim. Today I think it is a great idea to climb up and sit on the edge, while I sing and hum some songs to Jim until he falls asleep.

When I am certain Jim is sleeping, I try to get off the cradle without waking him up. As I wiggle off, my foot gets caught between the bars. I fall onto the floor and the cradle tumbles over me. I manage to wiggle my foot out, but the cradle is still up-side down on top of Jimmy. Stan tries to help me lift it up, but we can't push it back onto its rockers.

The blankets cover Jim's face and he is crying really hard. All of a sudden the noise stops. Worried that the baby is suffocating, I pinch him. Nothing. I start pulling the blankets and the pillow off his little body through the bars.

Finally, I hear Jimmy breathing and I don't even mind when he starts to cry again. I manage to pull him to the edge of the cradle, and he looks at me and Stan through the bars with his sad eyes as though we have done something bad to him.

I cannot get outside for help, we have no phone to call any-one, and I cannot lift the cradle, so I start to pray. "God help me, as I don't know what I am going to do for the rest of the day." Feeling guilty that I caused this accident, I continue to pray. "God keep Jimmy safe and healthy until Dad gets home."

All of a sudden I have this overwhelming feeling that God is listening to me and He is going to look after Jimmy and us. I feel God's hand is on my shoulder, and He is saying, "My child, eve-rything will be alright."

Stan and I sit on the floor beside the cradle until Jimmy falls asleep with his cheeks pressed against the bars. Later, while Jimmy is sleeping, we move to the table and do some more praying and we color birds. Stan is behaving exceptionally well and has been most helpful through the whole ordeal.

The smell coming from the cradle is strong and nauseating, but I am not able to change the baby for the whole afternoon until Dad gets home. I keep feeding Jim his bottle through the slots between the cradle bars, hoping this will help him to sleep more so the trauma of being trapped on the floor for hours will not be too much for him.

Dark is approaching, and the horse and wagon are in the driveway before I know it. I am banging on the window as hard as I can, to get Dad's attention before he unhitches the horse and starts feeding the animals. He always finishes his chores before opening the door for us, so he is not bothered immediately with details of our day.

Eventually, he notices me standing with Stan in the window and motioning to him to come quickly. He runs toward us and undoes the long bended nails, to discover a real emergency on the dirt floor. As he lifts the cradle and picks up the baby, he almost gets sick. The stink from the diaper is unbearable, but we are all happy that Jimmy is alright.

I have already drilled three-year-old Stan to be on my side and just nod to whatever I say to Dad about this incident. I tell Dad, "The cradle just fell all by itself, and we were not strong enough to lift it off baby Jim. We were just rocking Jim to go to sleep and it flipped over." Stan is looking at me and agreeing and I hope he won't say anything else.

Dad passes Jim over to me and commands, "Clean him up and we will talk about this when I finish my chores outside," as he shoots out the door like a bullet.

For this big washing job, I need to get a pail of water. When we purchased our property a few years ago it had no well. For the first couple of years, Mom carried fresh drinking water with two pails across her shoulders about two kilometers from the other side of town.

Grandpa searched for a water source all over the front and back of the property and finally found it on the hill in front of the house. My grandparents consider it a sacred place. Grandma often says, "God gives us this water to nourish our bodies and keep us alive. Our water has healing powers, so we drink a lot every day for our health."

The well is very big. The round shape is made out of cement blocks and has a flat top to rest our bucket on. It has a small wooden roof and a crank handle with a long chain attached to a large bucket. Grandpa taught me how to use it. "With a full bucket of water, the handle is extremely hard to crank," he explained, showing me how to tip it in for just a short time to fill it only halfway.

I feel blessed that Grandpa built the well low enough so I can fetch water for my Mom. I have to stand on a cement block so I can reach the bucket, but I can get it done.

Grandpa says some people are not as lucky as we are, with accessible fresh water. I think about Mom carrying the heavy buckets from the other side of town, and hope that we will have this good water springing from the earth forever, and know that we are blessed.

I am very happy that Jimmy is well and I don't mind cleaning him up. After he has been immersed in a tub full of warm water, he smells clean again. I can't seem to stop kissing him all over and singing to him.

God did tell me that everything will be okay with Jimmy, and I believed it. Whatever is coming to me from Dad, it can't be any worse than what I was feeling when the cradle toppled over onto Jimmy. I am ready for my punishment.

Chapter Eight

❧ ❦

My dad is a tall, slim, and handsome man with smiling blue eyes. His dark hair is long on top of his head and very short on the sides and back. Waves fall onto the right side, as he parts his hair on the left.

Dad can talk you in and out of anything and you want to listen to him for hours. He is very popular amongst his peers and is willing to have a drink with anybody. He treats everyone equally and has many, many friends who come over and take him out for drinks with them. His favorite is a shot of vodka straight up. Dad is a happy drunk, except with my mom. All his friends are willing to pay for his drinks, as he always pays his debts at harvest time.

Dad and Mom argue constantly about money. She reminds him that he pays for his drinking with our hard work during the entire year. Dad doesn't like hearing that, so they fight. Then he feels bad about it and he smashes things around and goes drinking some more. When he comes home, he is quite violent and physical with Mom and blames her for everything.

Now that Mom is gone, Dad is still drinking, but not as much as when she was here. Grandma refuses to babysit us at night when he goes out with his friends, so if he does go drinking I get to look after my brothers at night as well as in the day.

But at least there is no more fighting.

Some evenings Dad and I draw pictures together after the boys go to sleep. Drawing is the one passion I share with my Dad. He is very creative and he loves to draw and paint. In one of my memories, I am sitting with Dad on the bench under the cherry tree to study the birds and our animals. He says, "I will show you one special point to remember about them. We can sit down and draw after supper what we are observing now. Look at the colors and shapes and all the little details about them."

Dad's pictures are much nicer than mine, but he doesn't really have anyone else to show them to. He keeps drawing and showing me his techniques, and he teaches me how to make my pictures realistic. He says, "Pay attention to detail and how you can capture real shapes and colors."

I love this dad. I learn much from him and I wish he was like this all the time.

Other evenings, we have nice conversations about the farm and the animals, and sometimes about him and Mom. "Why does she always get angry with me and constantly call me a loser?" he wonders. "I work very hard on the farm, fixing things by myself and caring for all the animals. I need a drink once in a while to relax me." I just nod and smile and keep drawing.

After months of spending time with Dad, he is starting to make some sense to me. I am beginning to resent my mom for getting after Dad. I start to blame her for all of their fights, and I can hardly wait to tell her when she gets home.

☙ ❧

Finally, my dad is going to pick up Mom. He says, "We have to travel home with the new baby by train. It will be a long three days before we see you, so be good for Grandma."

Grandma comes over in the evening to help look after us. The next day, after they help us with the morning chores, Grandma and Grandpa must go to their farm and leave us all alone once again. But when they get home in the late evening, Grandma cooks a nice dinner for us. Grandma's favorite is pork hamburgers and lots of pepper all over everything. I am glad I don't have to peel and cook potatoes again.

When Mommy comes home from the hospital, I hardly recognize her. She has lost lots of weight and looks very thin, and her hair has been cut short. She has brought our baby sister with her. Mom loves the Virgin Mary, so she named my sister after her. Baby Mary is very small and sleeps all the time.

Mom boils water for all of us to bathe. I get in first with a blue cap covering my hair, so it won't get wet. After I dry myself, I supervise my brothers' bath time. They are both together in our round galvanized tub sitting by the potbelly stove to keep warm. They are splashing around having fun and they make lots of noise. Now I have more to clean up after their bath.

All of a sudden we hear a scream. Mom is squeezing our baby sister against her chest. Mom's eyes are as big as saucers and full of tears. Her mouth is wide open and she is screaming.

Dad walks over to Mom slowly, to see what is happening with baby Mary. Mom starts praying very loud, "Lord, forgive us for our sins, don't take this baby away from me." Dad gently takes my sister into his arms, lays her in the crib, and walks outside.

We are not sure what is happening. Mom curls up on the bed, sobbing. "Poor little Mary, only a few days in this world and she is taken away by the angels who brought her."

I take the boys out of the tub onto a blanket and try to dry them off. "Stop wiggling around, Jim. And Stan," I shout, "quit rolling on our dirt floor. You guys are getting dirty again." Finally they are in their pajamas and are sitting at the table getting snacks before bed. Jim is two years old now, and it is hard for me to carry him to his small chair. At six years old, I am not that strong.

Mom stays in bed, and keeps repeating, "I wish I was dead instead of baby Mary."

Our sister is dead.

When Dad comes back in, he says to me, "Your mother is sick with grief, and she is very weak from recent surgery. I have to do my outside work and tend to the animals. It will be up to you to look after your brothers, again, and cook and tend to our family."

Mom is not going to be available for a long while. I need to do my best for my brothers, and for her.

❧ ❦

On Sunday, everyone lines up to pass the white coffin. Our aunts and uncles are over to give their condolences, and Mom is just standing rigid and doesn't say a word. They are pushing me toward the casket, but I am afraid to look. I don't know my sister and I have never even held her, not even once.

Grandma is nudging me to keep going in this procession by the coffin, but I hang back. I think I am afraid of death. Finally, after everyone walks by, I start to move forward. I look at my sister's lifeless little body with her tiny head and very small hands lying peacefully. I feel very uneasy as I say, "Goodbye, Sister."

The next morning, Mom and Dad and the baby Mary drive off in our wagon and that is the last I see of my baby sister.

Grandma is helping to look after us in the evenings again. After three days, Dad comes home. He left Mom in the hospital to get better.

When Mom finally comes home, she is weak and sad. It seems no matter how much I help, she doesn't get better. Then one day, as I am doing the chores and trying to keep my brothers quiet, I see Mom doubling over with pain. I help her get on the bed to rest. "A glass of water would help, my daughter," she says. I bring her water and she finally lies down. She is so weak and pale that I am very worried. I hear her mumbling something as she fades away. "My sister, my sister . . ." Yes! Auntie will know what to do.

I put a cold cloth on Mom's head and run out the door as fast as I can. Auntie Kazia lives near our school, so I take a shortcut over the big hill. I hope Mom will be alright until we get back, as it is a long way from here.

Passing the old farm house on the right side of the gravel road, I see three additions with three different colors. The trail toward the house is very narrow, lined with thick grasses and tall bushes. Walking past this place always gives me the creeps. Something moves in the bushes and I yelp with fear.

Gravel is getting into my sandals as I start to run for my life. My mom is sick and I need to get to her sister's place, as Auntie will know how to help her. I can't think about the bush and the noise coming from it. I keep running, and finally make it to my aunt's place, out of breath.

"Slow down, my child," says Auntie Kazia. "What is wrong?" She looks down. "And what have you done to your foot?" Crouching to look, she removes a small rock that was grinding inside my sandal.

"Auntie," I gasp, "I was too frightened to stop. Something rattled in your neighbor's yard and scared me."

She looks at me with compassion and says, "Our fields around here are green and lush, and the vegetation is quite high. Sometimes they make swooshing noises. But Krysia, it's nothing to be scared about." She puts her hands on my shoulders. "It is nice to see you. But tell me, why are you here?"

"My mom is sick and I don't know what is wrong with her. She is weak and very pale. She was calling for you before I left. Please come and help her."

"After I wash and bandage your foot, we will go and see her. Don't worry, she will be fine. She is a very strong lady and a survivor, and she will live a long life, mark my words."

As we are walking past the big farm, I hear the noise again. "There it is," I say.

Auntie is holding my hand, and she smiles at me. "See, it is just the wind," she confirms.

We finally get to my house and I run to see how Mom is doing. As soon as Mom sees her older sister, she feels much better.

Thank you, God.

Gradually, Mom gets a little stronger. And soon, it is time for me to begin school.

Chapter Nine

Chickens and other animals run around in our back yard. In one corner of the yard we have a big manure pile with a hole at one end for the pissy liquid to drain into. That deep hole is there all year around and Dad keeps adding more manure every couple of days when he cleans the barn.

Today is a beautiful sunny day and we've just come home from church. Mom wants to cook a chicken for supper and is pleading with Dad to go and kill one of our chickens. Dad says, "That chicken didn't do nothing wrong, so I am not going to kill it."

After some not so nice words between Mom and Dad, Mom finally goes to do the job. Mom lays the chicken on the stump and holds it by the head. She swings the axe over the chicken's head and hits the neck slightly. Now this poor chicken is flapping all over the yard. I am crying and yelling, "Don't kill our pet chicken," as Mom is chasing it with an axe. Finally the chicken gets the last blow and rests on the stump. Dinner in the evening is difficult to swallow and no one wants to eat it.

Mom tries her best as a cook, but she was never taught cooking or any other skills except how to tend the garden. Although she dreamed of entering a convent and becoming a nun, she was pulled out of school before she could finish grade three and forced to help with her sister's kids and tend their big garden on a daily basis. Her sister, Auntie Kazia, told her school was not necessary for her future. "Your destiny is to be a farmer's wife, work on the farm, and have many babies."

After lunch, Auntie Kazia has come over to visit along with my cousin Josef, so we go outside to play. Josef suggests we go and smell the "hole" and see the creatures that live in there. We bend down on our bellies to see if anything alive is floating in the liquid. Josef says, "These creatures are very small, and we practically have to be touching the liquid with our noses to see them."

As we lie on our bellies and put our faces lower, almost touching the foul-smelling fluid, he pushes my face down and my nose touches the liquid. The smell is unbearable. I am worried I'll get it in my nose as probably it will make me very sick.

When my parents see me all dirty and stinky, they want to give both of us the strap. My gagging, spitting, and crying finally convince them that it isn't my fault. I was only interested to see what lives in there and what it looks like.

After Josef receives a spanking from his mom, they go home. I am very upset that I fell for his dumb ideas once again. He is always getting into mischief or getting someone else into trouble. He does like to joke around, but often he gets himself in hot water.

A few days later, we hear a knock on our door. It is Auntie Kazia. Josef is in the hospital and has lost his left leg. A machine to mill grain is in their back yard. The kids are not allowed to play around it, but yesterday he was chasing the horse that was pulling the machine and he slipped and got caught in the mill.

It will be very difficult for my seven-year-old cousin to have only one leg for the rest of his life. We all say a prayer for him and his family. Now, I am feeling horrible for thinking bad things about him for what he did to me last weekend.

Great-Grandma lives less than a block from my school, and I stop to see her often on my way home. Great-Grandma is always covered up and has a white complexion and skinny arms. The skin is hanging on her fingers, but her inviting smile melts my heart. She always greets me with a big smile and says, "How is my most beautiful girl?" Those words will echo in my head for days after I see her.

Great-Grandma lives in the barn, a tiny room with a cement floor. She had eleven children, and her youngest son built a big new house and a new barn for his family on her old property. There are a lot of small rooms in the barn for his animals and one room is for his mom, my great-grandma. Her son's wife doesn't want my great-grandma in her new house and does not want to have to care for her. She insisted that he put his mom in the barn where old people belong.

The cement floor is very cold in the summer, and Great-Grandma covers the floor with hay in the winter to keep it warmer.

Today Great-Grandma is sitting on the small bed in one corner and has a tiny table with two unmatched chairs in the other corner. In the middle of the floor she has a large scale to weigh the cherries she sells each day to kids after school. Her son has given her one cherry tree and tells her to pick and sell her cherries so she has a donation for Sunday mass. Great-Grandma will stand at her street corner for hours with her perfectly washed cherries, just to make a couple of dollars for the church offering. She is a very hard-working lady. She is very frail and can hardly walk as she is 89 years old, but she has a strong will to live. She makes people feel good with her ready smile for everyone.

The smell in her room, which is next to the horses and cow stalls, is awful as usual, but I guess she has gotten used to it. She never complains about where she lives. Her long black skirt drags on the dirty floor and the bugs are flying in her eyes. Maybe some of the smell is coming from Great-Grandma. I don't know how often she is allowed to go to her son's big brick house to wash. I know she has a big pail in her room to go to the bathroom in and it sometimes smells, too.

I am amazed at how she stoops and groans when she is getting up off the floor, but she never complains about her aches and pains. She gets off the bed, picks up a handful of fresh cherries and tells me, "Have a sit and eat. I picked them earlier today."

Cherries are my favorite of all the fruit we grow. These are my first this summer and I am dying to taste them. I pop a couple of them in my mouth and close my eyes, and my head explodes in a wonderful sensation with a great rich taste. Dark red juice runs down my throat and I forget where I am. When I open my eyes, we are sitting in Great-Grandma's doorway. The blue sky is beautiful, the fruit trees are moving slowly, being brushed by the wind, and I can smell her place once again.

As I leave for home, we hug in a tight embrace and she whispers in my ear, "Come back and see me tomorrow. Do not tell anyone about the free cherries. I have way too many great-grandchildren, and if they heard about this, they would be here every day. You are my favorite great-granddaughter and you appreciate my cherries a lot more than others."

"I promise not to tell anyone," I say. We smile at each other as we wave goodbye.

Great-Grandma is my mom's stand-in mother. Mom's mother has lived in Canada since I was six months old, so Great-Grandma is our grandma. She cares about me and she always has nice things to say to me.

Sometimes she tells me, "Don't be upset with your mom, she can't help when she is sick," and then she smiles at me. Her advice makes going home easier, for a time.

Chapter Ten

The hum of the train as it sits in the station being loaded is suddenly shattered by a loud whistle and, with a roar, the engines spring to life. The train rattles and shakes as it starts down the tracks.

Shaken out of my memories of the life I am leaving behind, I wiggle my body into a more comfortable position. As I settle into my seat, I look back outside and see many people I don't know who are waving to us. I am glad for a moment that they are all strangers. No one will recognize me and tell my parents I left on the train. Most people do not pay attention to kids like me.

The train ride is exciting and scary. I wonder where all the other passengers are going, where they came from. Maybe some, like Dad's cousins, have come all the way from America.

It is a nice summer day, and we are all working hard as usual. All of us are at home, exhausted, as the evening sky turns orange, when we hear a knock on the door. One of Dad's cousins announces that two older ladies from America are coming to town tomorrow for a visit. She explains that they are our second cousins, whom we have never met before. She tells us everyone is anxious to stop by to meet them and check them out at our uncle's place tomorrow after church.

It is impossible to get a good night's sleep because we are so excited to meet these distant relatives from so far away. To us, they might as well be from the moon. As we approach our uncle's place the next day, people from the whole town are waiting outside to see these ladies, to speak with them, and even to touch them. They are breathing the same air as we are, but the masses still want to see them face to face. No one in our town has traveled by airplane. Some people say the airplane is the devil's work, and others say it is some kind of miracle. Everyone is amazed that they keep people up in the sky instead of falling down to the ground.

Me, well, I am seven years old and not sure what to think of all these adults and their beliefs. It does seem funny how everyone is fussing over these two ladies and asking very odd questions. After the introductions, the women mostly visit with parents and other adult relatives, and they ignore us kids completely.

They look like any other adult to me, and they talk about church a lot—how people in America don't believe in the Catholic religion and follow the customs like we do here in Poland. They talk about how people work to make a living and dismiss the townspeople's belief that in America, money grows on the trees.

After a while, I go outside to play with my cousins and leave the boring stuff to adults. I sit on a wooden bench under a big tree, and I think about the things my relatives from America are saying. Is it true there is a place far, far away where people are just like us, but different? Most of them live different lives and speak different languages but still have to work for a living. Is it true the jobs are much easier to come by and the opportunities are endless?

What about the lemons we get from California? Do people in America witness the lemons growing? We only get them once a year in our town. Tomorrow is the day.

We have heard for months about them coming. Tonight, before they are about to arrive, we will stand in line in the cold and dark until tomorrow morning. We don't want to miss them.

After standing for hours and waiting for this golden fruit, it will be our turn to go inside the store. After the box is gently unpacked, the store owner, Mr. Waski, will only sell one lemon to each customer. "These lemons are like magic and promise to transport you to another place," he will say. Each year, Mr. Waski wants everyone in town to taste this foreign fruit and have this special experience. And the whole town will confirm that the lemons that come from America hold a special moment of unattainable gold.

The idea of America is very foreign and unreachable to all of us. We cannot imagine what is like over there, what kind of trees they have, and what kind of people live there. Even after talking to the women from America, some people still insist that America is a rich country where money grows on trees. But I don't believe it.

Today we are waiting in anticipation for the priest to show up and bless our house and everything in it.

Each year the Christmas tree is left in the house until the first or second week in February for the priest to bless it. I don't understand why. No one explains this ritual to us. Our parents just say, "That is the way we do things." Some people's trees catch on fire by the time the priest comes in February.

Our tree sits in the middle of the room, across from the pot-belly stove. We have to water it every day because it is dry, and the needles fall down on our dirt floor. It is hard to get all the needles off the floor. I have to sweep them daily with our corn broom.

Earlier this morning we went to church for the service. When we came home we cleaned the house, made our two beds, swept the dirt floor, and put a white cloth on the table. We only do that when someone special is coming over to visit. Today the very special person is the priest. Everyone in our town looks up to him and treats him like God. People fear him and I don't know why. We respect our priest for who he is, what he does, and what he stands for, but it seems to me that we shouldn't be afraid of him.

I put on my best church dress and white socks and tie blue ribbons in my pigtails. I do not have nice shoes to wear. We hope he will not look way down and notice the small holes in them. My brothers are wearing clean clothes, too.

We put out some cakes and tea and sit and wait for the priest to show up. Sometimes he arrives a few hours later than estimated, so after a while the boys go outside to play and get dirty, and we have to change their clothes again.

Looking at our tree, I am concerned that our handmade decorations are not good enough. We made them from catalogues and brochures relatives brought over to us to use as toilet paper. Dad was worried we wouldn't have enough paper. We cut those strips and glued them into connecting circles all one evening. He constantly reminded us, "You are going to run out of that shiny toilet paper if you are not careful and frugal with it." But now our tree is packed with decorations.

Finally, our neighbor comes over and says she has seen the priest two doors over, so he should be at our place soon. We make fresh tea, double-check our outfits to be sure everyone is nice and clean, and sit and wait some more.

The front door opens; the priest and another man who has been walking through the town with him come in. The priest is wearing a long-sleeved black gown that goes down to his feet. He has a white overcoat with a lacy bottom and long sleeves with lacy ends and a square neckline. On his head sits a large black hat with four corners and a tassel on the top. A long chain with a cross on it hangs around his neck.

After the greetings are over, the priest sits down and asks us kids, "Have you been good?" All three of us nod and say uh-huh, and he smiles at us and says, "That's good." He takes a bite or two of Mom's cake, then stands up and uses a small wand with a silver handle to sprinkle the four corners of our house with holy water. I am looking at the water going everywhere and am not sure what is going on.

The priest sprinkles his water on our Christmas tree. He says something in Latin and makes the sign of the cross with his left hand. Mom puts some money in his hand and he says, "Thank you for the cake and tea, your tree is very nice." Bowing his head, he says goodbye and leaves.

The whole ritual with the priest has taken less than 10 minutes and our lives go back to normal. We take the tree and the decorations down until the next year, when we get to do this all over again. Dad says, "We look forward to the priest's visit and his blessing each year. He renews our strength in our belief."

≈ ≪

A few days later I am getting ready for my First Communion. Grandma spits on both my brothers' hair to make it lie down. "Stand still, and quit fussing about," she yells. They both squeal and run away.

My hair is very fine and flyaway, and when I wake up, it stands straight up and is full of static. Most days I curl my hair on wires wrapped with cloth before going to bed. My mom is not into doing things like that for me. "It is up to you to look decent the next day for school and on Sunday morning for church," she insists. Most girls have nice wavy hair and their moms help them to look good. My mom says, "If you want to curl your hair it is up to you; I wouldn't bother with it."

Grandma braids my hair into two pigtails and intertwines them with beautiful white ribbons. She puts a crown made of fresh flowers on my head. "You look like a princess today," she says, adding, "Don't dirty your white dress."

As we walk to our church for this special occasion, I am careful not to play with my brothers as they run around and play hide-and-go-seek. I don't want to dirty the new dress that Grandma bought for me. I am excited and somewhat frightened, not knowing what to expect.

We are ushered toward the front of the church and kneel down in front of the priest. He speaks Latin and prays for us, but I don't understand any of it. He gives me my first piece of skinny wafer called Holy Bread and puts it on my tongue. It feels very light and has no taste. I am not sure what to do with it. Should I swallow it or chew it? I roll the Holy Bread in my mouth until it melts.

"Now you need to go see the priest for your first confession," Grandma says.

As I step into the confessional room, I am scared of what he might say or do to me when he hears my sins. When I report to him about getting angry at my mom or my brothers he might not like me. I don't like this part of First Communion.

After I tell the priest everything, he is quiet for a moment. Then he says, "You need to do five Hail Marys and stay out of trouble." He makes the sign of the cross over his chest with his right hand and walks out of the confessional booth. I kneel for a few seconds longer, talking to God about forgiving me for all the things I told the priest. Finally, I stand up and walk out but I feel confused.

My family comes over and gives me hugs. They tell me, "You are a big girl now. From now on, you get to see the priest every Sunday and tell him all your sins."

Chapter Eleven

ॐ ॐ

One day while I am visiting Grandma, I tell her I want to make some notes about the birds and butterflies. She gives me Grandpa's tattered old notebook. My eyes cannot believe it. My own notebook! I press it to my chest like a big treasure and say, "I will never let you go."

I tell her, "I see our apples grow and change size and color and finally fall out of the trees. They change from a beautiful white flower to sweet, delicious apples we eat. Some days I see bees on the apples, but I run away."

"Did you know that bees know if you are scared of them?" Grandma asks, and I shake my head no.

"I will be recording things every day and read it to you later on if you like," I offer, and she almost smiles.

I watch how butterflies are made and how beautiful they are. I ask Grandma, "How do they make themselves from a slug to a beautiful butterfly? And Grandma, there are so many birds outside. How do they talk to each other and to their babies?"

She smiles and says, "One day you will have all the answers; don't rush it, my child, don't rush it."

Ever since I can remember, I have wanted to write notes about everything, and I seem to have something to write about everywhere I go. Paper is not easy to get and we are not allowed to write on our school papers, so I have only been able to use scraps, and I am always afraid of losing them and all of my important observations. Now, I am so proud of my notebook from Grandma. I take it everywhere I go.

∽ ⤳

Tonight I went to get my notebook and it was gone. I left it on the table when I went out to feed the chickens. I think maybe my brother took it and tore it up or threw it somewhere. I turn all the household stuff upside down looking for it, to no avail.

Dad asks me, "Why are you walking around with your head hanging to the ground?" After I tell him I lost my important writing pad he confesses, "I didn't know it was that important. When I came home from work I saw the pad on the table with some writing that didn't make sense, so I took it to use it in the bathroom. I knew it wasn't school work and I am very sorry. You will get another notebook and write more stories later."

Dad doesn't understand that I cannot capture the same things the next time.

In the morning I tell Grandma, "I have lost my notepad and all my important notes, and I don't know what to do now."

Grandma looks at me. "Sometimes you have to stop worrying, wondering, and doubting," she says. "Have faith that things will work out, maybe not how you planned, but just how it's meant to be." She gives me a big hug. "This too shall pass."

Somehow I feel much better and I do hope I will get a new notepad soon.

After that incident, I hide all my special things in my hiding place behind the tall dresser under my bedding. Sometimes I bury things under the cherry tree by the fence in a tin can where no one would look for them.

The air is thick and I feel unsettled and restless. A gloomy mist hangs over our back yard after the rainfall. The sky is dark grey and promises a housebound day.

Mom has been home for the last few days. She was away at the hospital for a long time, and when she finally came home, she brought with her my little baby brother. She is happy again and the baby seems to be fine, except for the occasional cough. He has beautiful blue eyes and wavy blonde hair. Mom named him Mark. He is a happy baby and smiles a lot.

Today Mark is very quiet. He almost looks sad and is not smiling as usual.

For the past few days, we have had lots of visitors. Our cousins and aunts and uncles and some friends are happy to see my mom and the baby. The house is busy and much chatter is going on every day.

Today, the baby started a coughing spell and he can't seem to stop. Stan and Jim and I are sitting in the corner being quiet. Mom looks very worried about what is happening to little Mark, and her face is white like a ghost. I start praying for Mark to live. "Please God, keep our baby brother strong and healthy and don't let him die."

After a while, the baby is still coughing and getting weaker. Mom is crying and praying a lot. She doesn't want to do anything else except look after Mark. I try to be helpful and also look after my brothers.

Auntie Ginny is visiting us today. She congratulates Mom and walks over to the crib, then calls for Mom, very alarmed. "Gabby, something is wrong with your baby and his eyes are rolling back," she says. Mom screams and runs over to the crib and picks up the baby as he closes his eyes for good.

"Oh, God, not again, don't let me lose another child," Mom wails. She keeps praying and crying, and we stand there and don't know what to do. Mom lies down on her bed with our baby brother and holds him close to her chest and continues to pray. "Please God, don't let him die."

Grandma comes over after she hears Mom's screams and says, "I will call the doctor for help; you will be fine," and she disappears.

Auntie feels bad for Mom, but she goes home and leaves me to look after Mom again. I put a cold cloth on her forehead and hold her hand. Mom is still holding the baby and won't let go.

Dad gets home a couple of hours later and discovers what has happened. He is sitting very quietly and keeps looking at the baby. He lets out a big sigh and says, "They kept opening all the windows on the train and the baby caught something."

"It could be the wrong blood they gave me at the hospital," Mom says, sobbing.

Mom is talking about the blood transfusions she received earlier. She lost lots of blood by the time Dad took her to the train station and then to the hospital. She also blames the cold draft from the open windows on the train when they were coming back from the big city. After she noticed the baby sneezing and coughing on the train, she kept closing the windows.

She blames our house, with its damp dirt floor and all the smells coming from the animals walking around by our front door. And she even mentions me and my two brothers breathing on the new baby and constantly touching his little hands.

I wish I could take it all back so our baby brother could still be alive.

The next day, Dad leaves the house early in the morning to make arrangements for the funeral. He comes home later with a white coffin.

Relatives keep coming over, bringing cakes and shaking my parents' hands and everyone is very sad and praying for Mom.

I don't want to be here, so I go outside to sit under the cherry tree and write on a piece of paper about what is happening in the house. Teddy is barking, as he is not used to seeing so many people, and I call him over and cuddle him.

Evening has come and all the people have left. Dad announces that he is taking the coffin tomorrow morning and putting it in the grave with our sister who died sixteen months ago.

I keep asking Dad, "Where is the grave?" He doesn't say much about that. He just keeps saying, "Get back to work, we don't want to dwell on these things any longer."

Mom is very distressed and upset. She cries every time we look at her. I am seven years old and have a lot of responsibility already, and now I must continue to take care of Mom. My brothers are five and three now, and they like to play a lot and don't listen to me very well. They know something is wrong, but they don't know what is happening or why Mom is crying all the time.

After everyone goes home, I take Mom's hand and we walk to the statue of the Virgin Mary. I bring a candle and matches, and we light it for my dead baby brother as we did awhile back for my baby sister when she died. We sit and pray.

Mom is crying again, and I hold her and tell her, "Everything will be okay, Mom, because baby brother is in Heaven with baby sister and all the angels." She looks at me so sadly and nods, and I think I see a small smile in the corner of her mouth. "As long as you are home with us, Mom, everything will be okay."

Chapter Twelve

We have a big, round portable tub where Mom washes our clothes and where we have our baths. The only thing I have to look forward to is washing dishes, wringing clothes and helping with baths for my brothers. At least I am working with my mom.

I wait for Saturday to come so Mom and I can talk a little when we both bathe Jim and Stan. I hold up the towel so the boys won't splash around too much and make mud in our house.

Saturday is also the family wash day before we go to church on Sunday. Everyone and everything gets washed, not like during the week when only faces and hands, and occasionally our feet, get washed before bedtime.

The tub gets filled with hot water from the huge pot sitting on the stove all day getting warm. I am the oldest so I bathe first, then Stan and Jim. Mom and Dad bathe last and I am pretty sure it is in the cold, dirty water after we go to bed. Our parents hang a long white sheet from the ceiling so we can't see them bathe.

On Sunday morning we all walk to church and the priest has a special service for baby Mark. Dad says, "After the service we will all go to the cemetery and I'll show you where I have buried your sister and brother." The cemetery is a short distance behind the church. I am scared but interested to see where they are.

When we get to the cemetery, I scan the graves around me and see two small graves with no names. "I wonder how we are going to know later who is in them."

Dad looks at me and says, "Do not worry, we will get small stones engraved with their names later on." Mom crumbles with pain when she hears us talking about the stones. She sits on the ground trying to regain her composure.

We are all very sad standing in the cold, as Dad picks up Mom and motions for me. "Grab the boys' hands and get back on the road; we got to get going."

I worry how Mom is going to walk home in her condition. She looks weak and she has not been eating for the past few days since Mark's death. It is very painful to see her like this.

We finally make it home and I put Mom to bed and cook supper for us. I have sent Dad to the store to get a few things. The store is not too far so he should be home soon. I have cleaned the house and fed the boys and then I realize he has been gone a long time.

Mom is lying down and moaning but she can see the boys. I put Jim to bed and give Stan some coloring to keep him busy. I tell Mom, "I will be right back." Then I walk toward the store to see what has happened to Dad.

I can't believe what I see. Dad is stumbling home, tripping over the cobblestones and singing. He staggers into a horse and carriage driving in the opposite direction and falls to the ground. I run to pick him up and we walk the rest of the way home.

As we approach the house, Dad tells me he wants to go into the barn and sleep with his horse. "Your mom is going to yell at me. I didn't shop at the store, and I drank the money." He starts to cry.

"Everything will be okay, Dad," I tell him. "Mom is asleep and you need to rest." I don't know how long we have been sitting on the bale of hay by the barn with me holding him in my arms, but it feels good.

We walk in quietly. I put Dad on the bed and take his boots off and tuck him in. I put Stan to bed early.

Mom lifts her head. "What is happening?"

"Go back to sleep," I say. "Everything is good," and I cover her and give her a kiss on the cheek. I climb into my bed behind the dresser without supper and start to pray for my parents.

I am taking the back road from school today. It has more hills than our regular flat road but is a bit shorter. Auntie Barbara lives on top of the hill up the road from my school. I see her working in the garden as usual. She shouts to me, "Come over and have some tea and cookies."

I can smell the gingerbread as I approach her kitchen. She is always very nice to me and reminds me again, "We are relatives, so it is good for us to visit together." She has a nice, inviting smile.

Her daughter, Teresa, who is around 30 years old, always looks sad. I know something is not right with her, as she sits with us and doesn't say a word.

As usual, Auntie Barbara asks me a lot of questions. "How is your school?"

"School is fine."

"What would you like to do when you grow up?"

"I would like to move to a big city and work there. If I can find something I am good at."

She smiles. "You can be bad at something, Krysia, but if you love doing what you are doing that will be enough." She pours the tea. "How is your mom doing?"

"She is doing much better. But she is still very weak and needs lots of rest and she doesn't do much with us kids."

Auntie Barbara took over this old house with its many small rooms after her parents died. Her husband was killed during World War II and Auntie is left with her only daughter, Teresa. They are two lonely women living together, and they never go anywhere.

Thank God their patch of land is behind their house so they don't have far to walk. They have many fruit trees in front of the house and keep very busy drying and storing fruit for the winter. Also, they store all their vegetables in a big cellar under the house.

I say goodbye, knowing I will have to walk home quickly so I don't get in trouble with my mom for being late from school.

The following week, I am coming home from school as usual and I see Auntie Barbara sitting outside on the bench beside her favorite tree. She is crying, and I want to keep going and not disturb her. But she notices me and motions for me. "Come over, Krysia, come see me for a little while."

I am not sure what to do. When my mom is crying I just go outside until she is finished. But I join Auntie on the bench, and she tells me, "I came home the other day from the store and my Teresa was gone."

"Where did she go?" I ask.

"I don't know, and her note says that she is never coming back and not to look for her."

I close my eyes and take a deep breath. What do I say to that? I cannot think of anything. Heat is collecting in the inner creases of my elbows and in the soft places behind my knees. I finally let out my breath and realize I have been holding it for a while.

I open my eyes and I nod and put my arms around Auntie's neck. I hold her tightly for what seems like hours and tell her, "Everything will be alright."

She smiles through her tears and says, "Thank you for being here with me."

We say a prayer for Teresa's wellbeing and I leave for home.

When I get home, Grandpa tells me, "They found Teresa's body in the ditch about five kilometers from her house."

"I wonder where she was going," I say. But no one has ever been able to find out what happened.

A few days later at Teresa's funeral, I see my Auntie Barbara is very sad. I walk over and hold her hand and afterward I give her a big hug. We walk to her house after the funeral and the food prepared by her neighbors is very tasty. It is nice to see she has many friends and family to support her in this difficult time.

Tomorrow I will visit Auntie Barbara after school and we will sit outside beside her favorite tree and she will tell me many stories from days gone by. She will share how lonely her life is all by herself. I most likely will share how lonely my life is with my unhappy mom, and we will hug each other. I can almost hear her shout, "See you soon, Krysia," as we wave our goodbyes.

Chapter Thirteen

❧ ❧

As the train sways and slows down for another stop, I wonder if some of the other passengers are also running away from home. The lady sitting across from me has the nicest smile I have ever seen. Maybe she is going to visit her loved ones. She has been reading from a big book, but now she puts it away. As she gets off the train, she turns around to wave at me and says goodbye as if I am a friend.

Who is she? Where is she going? Does she have children, and how many? Who did she leave them with? I want to run after her and ask her to come back and sit with me. We could talk and laugh and play guessing games as we count the trees passing by.

Whenever I am upset, I count everything in sight. I count trees, weeds, flowers, clouds, rocks in our driveway, chickens chasing me. First I guess how many there are and then I count carefully and make sure I am right. Being right is very important in our family. No one ever says sorry; we just have to try harder next time.

⊱ ⊰

Most of the time I like to observe and study people just as much or more as I like to observe and study animals and nature. Today I am spending some time with my dad observing the clouds. He takes pride in telling me what kind of weather we will have tomorrow. He has learned how from Grandpa, who learned from his father, my great-grandfather, who used to be the town's weatherman.

"Tomorrow will be a sunny day with some light rain in the evening," he says.

"How do you know that?" I ask.

"See those big pillow-soft clouds and how they are breaking up into a thin strip?" Whatever is up there he is able to interpret to me, and it seems his prediction is always right. I am very proud of my dad. He is gentle and kind to all our animals and I hope I have these qualities when I grow up. He works very hard, and he reads Grandpa's books. He is quite smart and my only wish is that he didn't drink so much.

One day, when we are on our way to our plot of land, I am complaining about it being too far to walk. Dad says, "Walking clears your head of dumb thoughts and it will relax your mind. You will be able to observe more of what is around you—the smell of the fields, the acres of planted vegetables, and the beauty of nature. Don't forget to look up and see a beautiful sky, ever-changing as we walk. The rain is coming tomorrow to wash things clean."

The next day we are walking that same road and the ground is dry but the smell of the grain after the rain is strong. Dad says, "Let's sit down and rest a little." We close our eyes and breathe the fresh air around us and pretend we are floating through space. I like this dad and I like these peaceful moments with him.

I think of Mom, and of my vague memories of my parents having happy moments together when I was small. Mom seems so sad and unhappy all the time now, but I know that a long time ago she had dreams for the future, when she was young like me.

I am worried about our lives now that Mom is home, because she is distant and void. She doesn't speak much to us kids, or Dad, or our grandparents. She usually keeps working from dusk to dawn on the farm and later in the house. I don't know how to fix things so she can be happy again. I just want our lives to be like they were before Mom started being sick and having more babies.

I am learning that most of the time my life is influenced by my mom, her moods and activities, her love or lack of it, good or bad, troubled or peaceful, hard or easy, happy or not.

Mom has often told me about how she wanted to be a nun for as long as she could remember. "I was not allowed to go to the nunnery and serve God," she says, with tears in her eyes. "My sister needed me to babysit her kids and help out on the farm."

Now, Mom wants me to go to the convent to serve God when I grow up. She has the idea that nuns don't do very much, only pray all day. "Don't get married, my daughter," she says. "I was forced to get married by my mom and my sister. We were not made to be work horses. Serving God is all you need to do, and that kind of life will be much easier." Then she turns away and starts humming our Christian songs. This is Mom's escape. Whenever she is troubled, uncomfortable, or hurting, singing gives her another space to be in.

But the more my mom talks about me being a nun, the more I resent her. I want to be a normal girl like all my friends. And I think she resents me and my brothers, too. "I didn't want to get married or have any children," she tells us quite often. The first time I heard that, I was very confused and scared. I thought I should not have been born or that she doesn't want us.

The longing for my mom's affection upsets my tummy a lot. I am always looking at Mom, trying to get more hugs out of her, but she is not much for that. Mostly she is just in a lot of turmoil and pain.

My animals are my sanctuary. I sing to them for distraction. Sometimes singing works and sometimes it doesn't. I don't really want to think about what Mom is saying about being a nun. I know my mom loves me and my brothers, but she is lost in herself. She mourns her lost babies and takes the blame for their deaths. "I was sick and weak most of my childhood," she says. "That's why they died."

Some days it seems she doesn't even notice us kids and Dad. Often she looks like she is travelling somewhere else. On occasion, she looks right through us like she is trying to figure out who we are or where she is.

ॐ ॐ

We still live next door to Grandma Kula and I talk to her a lot. She tells me, "You can come over anytime you want because you are my favorite granddaughter."

I say, "I am your only granddaughter, Grandma."

Grandma invites me to her side of the house for tea and biscuits, but no one else is invited. I don't want to leave Mom all alone, and she doesn't want me to go over to Grandma's. I am very confused and never sure what to do.

Grandma asks, "How is your mom doing?"

I tell her Mom keeps talking about being a nun.

Grandma just shakes her head and says, "Don't worry about it, everything will be fine. I will teach you how to cook and bake and all sorts of things in the kitchen." I nod and smile and give her a hug. But Grandma always tries to persuade me to take her side and says things like, "Your mother doesn't understand much of life, and we'd best leave her alone."

I want to feel good about my mom and I don't want her to go away again. I go back to Mom, and I tell her, "Don't worry yourself about any of the things Grandma is saying. She is provoking you and you don't need that. You need to pray and stay strong for us all. Everything will be okay, I promise." I make Mom a cup of chamomile tea.

One night, something startles me and I awake abruptly. I peek around the corner and see Dad cuddling up to Mom. As she feels his touches, she turns around and says, "Go away and don't bother me ever again. I don't want any more children that are going to die. I can't bear it anymore."

I see Dad move away from Mom and stare at the ceiling. Mom rolls over to the edge of the bed and closes her eyes. I can just imagine what she must be feeling. Living in this one-room hole with five of us, not much to eat—mostly potatoes and milk every day—getting pregnant, having kids and then watching them die.

She spends too much energy on trying to survive emotionally and physically. No wonder she can't bear it any longer. And she didn't want any of this, and her dreams of becoming a nun will never become reality. I can hardly wait to grow up and leave this place and have my own life. I will never live like this.

Chapter Fourteen

❧ ❧

My parents are still fighting all the time. Some days I have to try to ignore them while I am doing my homework. Other times, I run and hide in my cubbyhole behind the tall dresser while they are yelling and screaming at each other.

Mom always ends up crying, or she gets pushed or shoved or often punched in the stomach or her face. The ritual of fighting goes on almost daily. It is a terrible thing to see and listen to. It makes my skin itch, and sometimes I will scratch myself until I am bleeding. Their voices have sharp edges and get very loud. I have to put my fingers deep inside my ears so I won't hear the screaming. After the fight, Dad either stomps out of the house to go drinking some more or he passes out across their bed. Mom either goes to sleep with the boys or sits on the kitchen chair all night, wondering where he is.

Looking at my Mom's sad eyes, I see a secret buried deep inside. What is she not saying? This secret runs in our blood through generations. And I think I have figured it out: My mother doesn't know how to love and is mostly void, like her mother who left for days on end to sell vegetables in a big city while my mom's grandmother looked after her. I can see Mom still longs for her mother's love.

Right after my mom got married, Grandma Janiga traveled to Canada to join her husband. My mom does not remember her dad. She was six months old when he left to search for work.

Grandma Janiga had no opportunity to attend school. My great-grandma worked on the farm from dawn to dusk and left Grandma Janiga at a very young age to look after eleven siblings.

This has gone on for generations, and no real love has been passed on to the women in my past. I am determined to find out the whole story about the generations of women whose lives are defining my own.

~ ~

Thinking about my mom's dream of becoming a nun and serving God reminds me of a lady who lives not far from us. She seems to love God, too, but in a different way. In fact it makes people think she's kind of crazy. She's like my mom in another way, too. She is lonely and starved for love. But in other ways, they are quite different.

Mary is her name, and that is all I really know about her. She has a big square face like most of the ladies in our village. She is tall and has to bend down every time she goes in or out of her small one-room house. She lives alone on the other side of the river, and everyone says she is crazy. The townspeople also say she is a witch, because she comes up with some interesting and wild ideas about everything. "Only witches predict what will happen in our future," they say, "so stay away from Mary."

Sometimes, when I pass Mary's house to get across the small bridge to see my cousin Jana, who lives a few houses down the road from her, Mary waves and calls out to me. She says things like, "You are a child of God and He loves you and has a plan for your life." She frightens me a bit, but I always smile and wave and say, "Have a nice day, Miss Mary."

Today, as I cross the small bridge, I see Mary outside feeding her chickens. "Please come over," she calls. "I won't bite you."

Reluctantly, I step into her messy yard and she greets me with a big smile. "How are you, my child, and where are you going today?"

"To visit my cousin Jana and her neighbor, Ania the seamstress," I answer.

"Lovely day for a visit," she says. Then she invites me inside. I feel a bit nervous and fidgety. "Let's have some tea and cookies. Do you like cookies?"

I nod nervously. As Mary is making tea, she keeps smiling at me which puts me at ease.

The house has hardly anything in it: one small window with a lace curtain, a potbelly stove in the middle of the room, a small bed, a table with two different colored chairs and in the corner, a small stove to cook on. One corner has a pile of different kinds of books.

"You must read a lot," I say.

"It is not easy living in a small town like this," she says. "Folks call you crazy if you don't think exactly like they think. So I read." Her kettle whistles, and she brings tea and cookies to the table. Then she starts to prophesy to me. "One day you will travel far away from here. You are a very smart young lady and want to always learn things. Don't ever give that up."

"How do you know, Miss Mary?" I ask.

She shrugs and says, "I just know these things."

I have ignored most of her talk in the past, but this day something happens. I am listening and nodding and hoping that what she says is true.

I see now that she has a good heart. She is a lonely lady and just wants to talk with somebody. I don't think anyone stops and talks to her, and she tells me she has never been married and has no children of her own. Mary is starving for people's closeness, and I think she has a lot of knowledge. "People are not sure what to think of me," she says, "and what I say sometimes scares them. They call me a witch, you know."

I nod politely, feeling awkward because I have called her one, too.

After this visit, I see Mary in a different way and I am no longer afraid of her. In fact, I love listening to her and her ideas. I can't tell anyone I have spoken with Mary, and especially cannot talk about my visit inside her house. People in our community would have another person to point fingers at: me.

A few days later, I awake from a wonderful dream and I think about what she said. "One day you will travel the world." How does she know what will happen to me and my travels in the future? Has God revealed to her his plans for me? Or is she really a witch like everyone believes? I don't think so. I feel safe being with her, and she does give me a lot of ideas to think about.

I am going to see my cousin Jana, and I decide to go the shorter way again, past Mary's place, hoping to get a glimpse of her warm smile, showing off her long teeth. She is outside, wearing her full-size apron with flowers on it, and her hair is in a bun on the back of her head. She waves hello to me and I hurry across the small bridge to meet her.

Her eyes sparkle as she embraces me. "It is good to see you," she says. "How have you been lately?"

We sit outside on the two front steps as chickens peck all around us. On one side of her house she has a beautiful garden full of wonderful flowers, and some of them smell very nice.

"I will be a famous writer one day," I share with her.

She smiles and encourages me. "Keep that dream alive, always, and you will be one." We hug and I go on my way to my cousin's place.

I have never shared this kind of talk with any living soul. Occasionally, though, I find myself talking to my dead sister, Mary, and I tell her all my secrets. Now, I tell her about my visits to Mary "the witch," and her ideas about life. I know she won't tell anyone else.

I am lucky to have visited Mary a few times, as now I have heard she has died. I didn't even know she had been sick; she had never mentioned it to me. I will miss her spirit and the gentleness she showed to me. She was my friend. Now our townsfolk will find other things to talk about.

Chapter Fifteen

I can hardly wait to become a Girl Guide. I've heard so much about the club from other girls, how they get to help others, and now I want it to be my turn to help those less fortunate and get to do some walking to the neighboring villages and towns as a team.

This concept of working together as a Girl Guide is foreign to me, as my dad always says we should look after ourselves first. "Looking after others is a waste of good productive time," he says. "Those who have nothing to do join groups and teams and they eventually become very lazy. It starts with Girl Guides and the next thing you know you'll be part of some movement against your own family."

But today is my birthday and I have turned eight years old. I am old enough to be sworn in as a Girl Guide. I get to wear a grey uniform like the older girls. The badges I have to work for will be sewn on my uniform and worn with pride.

My teacher, Miss Agnes, understands my desire to be a Girl Guide, so she is sending a note to my parents for their permission for me to join. I will have a hard time convincing my dad as he is not in favor of us kids doing anything except our chores and homework after school hours. Also, it costs a dollar, which we don't have.

Grandma comes to the rescue after a long discussion with me. She knows how badly I want to join. I have promised to do everything I have to do on the days we have meetings, and to help Grandma with extra chores on the other days. She can see me agreeing to all the terms, and after thinking about how beneficial it will be for me to belong to this worthwhile group, she gives me the money. I can hardly sleep. Tomorrow, after classes are over, I will be sworn in.

The following week, we go for a walk with Miss Agnes in the woods behind the school. We are exploring and looking at all the different trees and pinecones. We gather some special cones for upcoming crafts so we can sell them later on and raise money for those who are really poor.

I notice the sun is very low as we navigate down the steep hill, and it is shining bright red through the trees. I fall in love with that picturesque view and I can hardly wait to get home to draw it. When we get back to school, I see the peaceful sun going down upon a wide pink sky. It has been a perfect day with my favorite teacher.

I run home very excited about my trip and the beautiful scenery I have experienced. I describe it to Dad and we draw it on a precious big piece of white paper.

The times spent as a Girl Guide are the best. We are very busy helping others less fortunate with their yard work, picking vegetables for them, picking fruit off the trees, looking for gooseberries, feedings animals, carrying food in the house, milking cows, and helping with other small jobs as they need.

❧ ❦

Mom's hair is long and black, and most of the time she has it braided and twisted into a bun. She smells like the chamomile she grows around the front yard for tea. Mom makes the tea very strong for rinsing her hair after shampooing it. She says, "Chamomile tea is good for whatever ails you." When we are not well, we drink the tea and gag, but the next day we feel much better.

I come in from outside and Mom says, "My goodness, look who's here, our famous writer."

I smile and ask her, "Would you like to see my latest writings? I have notes about the adventurous times I will be having with Auntie Veronica and my cousins one day." We sit down for a short while and she listens to my ramblings. Mom smiles and nods and I wish this time would never end.

It is late in the evening. My two brothers have been asleep for some time now, and I am doing my homework when I hear a loud voice and swearing coming from outside. Then someone is opening the door. I look at Mom and it seems like the life has drained out of her. She is standing still and bracing herself for another explosion.

At this moment I realize that at this late hour I had best not be seen awake or I'll get it too. While Dad fumbles to open the door and drops the key, I scoot to my little room behind the tall dresser. I am as quiet as a mouse when he enters the room.

I cover my ears so I don't have to hear exactly what Mom and Dad are saying to each other. She most likely has told him to be quiet so he doesn't wake up the whole neighborhood. Now they are both yelling at each other, and the air behind the dresser is getting thicker. I can hardly breathe so I start to pray. "Please Lord, help us all. Help my parents to love each other and keep them from any harm."

Grandma Kula usually comes over to intervene when my parents fight. I am sure she hears the banging and yelling going on, and I am waiting for her to barge in and grab Dad by the ear and pull him outside to give him a talking to. She has done this before and it seems to settle Dad. But not tonight

After what seems like hours, I hear Grandma banging on the adjoining wall and saying, "Enough Jozef, enough." Then I hear Dad swear and slam the door on his way out.

Dad has these blackouts when he is drinking, and the next day, he doesn't remember what he did. His friends feed him some kind of moonshine they make from who knows what. They know Dad would do anything for a drink. He doesn't care what it is made from as long as he gets drunk and numb.

I don't know what would have happened if Grandma didn't stop Dad. I am falling asleep finally, and Mom is moaning on her bed. I know she is still alive, but I am scared to come out and see what happened earlier. All of a sudden I hear a big bang and crash against the dresser that I am lying behind. Mom has fallen down on our hard dirt floor.

Dad must have come back in and grabbed her out of the bed and thrown her against the dresser. I hear him staggering around and then the front door opens. He stomps out again and slams the door behind him.

I don't hear any sound coming from Mom. Slowly I crawl out of my hiding spot and see Mom lying lifeless, bleeding on the floor. I scream, "Mom, Mom, please wake up," but she doesn't move. At this point I am very scared. I think I have lost her for-ever, this time.

I put a wet cloth on her bleeding head and I shake her slight-ly. "Mom, say something, please. God, please make sure she is still alive." She makes a faint sound like she is in excruciating pain. "Thank you, God, for keeping my Mom alive."

I wipe the blood above her eye, as it is running into her ear. She looks at me with her sad eyes and starts to cry. I hold her in my arms and tell her, "Everything will be alright. Come and sleep in the boys' bed, so when Dad returns later, he won't disturb you." She mumbles something as I pull her up on the bed.

I can recall, from when I was very young, my father being drawn to my mother like a moth to a flame. I have flashes from some happy, long-ago times. When did they begin to have a war against each other? I do know that the prisoners they are taking with them are us kids. My only answer is that one day I'll escape far from here.

I tuck Mom into bed with a cold cloth on her wound. She says, slurring, "He went back drinking some more and spending money we don't have."

"Shush, go to sleep." I sit beside her until she falls asleep and then I go to my sleeping cubbyhole.

I leave the lantern burning on the table so Dad can see when he gets back later.

When I wake up to the sun beaming through the windows, I see Dad passed out on his bed with his boots on. I wake up the boys quietly. "We need to scoot outside so we don't wake Dad up," I tell them. "He needs his rest."

Mom is lying motionless, so I shake her gently to make sure she is still with us. "I'll get you another cold cloth to put on your head, just rest. I love you, Mom."

I run to see Grandma. "Please get a doctor, to see if Mom is alright. Last night she was bleeding from her head and she is very weak."

Grandma looks at me sadly and gives me a hug. "Don't worry, my child, everything will iron itself out in the end," she says. But she promises to get the doctor.

I walk back to our side of the house. I see Dad lying dead to the world on one bed and Mom on the other bed moaning and groaning with pain.

Praying always helps me. "Lord, I just want my mom and dad to get along and be happy."

ॐ ॐ

My family and I are always active, walking everywhere. It is delightful when the wind is whistling and scattering beautiful leaves around. Clouds are moving fast like someone is driving a hundred horses behind them. Now the wind is bending our fruit trees and whistling in the chimneys, shaking our house so as to wake us up.

I glance at the sky above the trees, where the day is beginning to decline and the sunset will come soon. It is time to milk Babunia, and I have only done this chore once before with my Grandma's help. I see the sunset is very near, as I hear the horse and wagon coming toward me. My dad is driving home from the farm.

Dad walks into the barn and hears me singing as I hold the pail. He says, "We need to be quiet when Babunia is in the stall so we don't spook her. Be very gentle, and she will give you lots of milk. If you talk too loud it will make her nervous and scare her, and she won't give you any. And call her by her name, because she understands us."

The pail is large and Mom's gumboots are way too big for my feet, but they are the best to wear in the barn. I rest my body on Babunia's side as I sit on a very low stool. I straddle her milk bag and try to remember how to pull down on the udders to get milk. I once saw Mom squeezing Babunia's bag to see how full it was, so I start with that. She lifts her right hoof and knocks the pail over into the muck. I start to cry and Dad rushes into the barn to see what has happened.

"Start over again after you clean the pail," he says. "Second time lucky. Now, don't let Babunia have her way with you. And don't be afraid, just talk to her nice and soft and she will listen to you."

"I will," I mumble. After I clean the pail, I pull the stool closer and begin pulling down on the teats. I am speaking softly and calling her name, and to my surprise the milk starts coming out. I am very excited to see the milk coming and I keep pulling until there is no more.

I feel happy and very proud that I am able to get a pail full of milk. The sunset is shining red through our fruit trees and I pause to admire the wide orange sky. "Serene sunset, I look forward to seeing you again tomorrow."

Chapter Sixteen

Early on a cold and windy morning, Mom announces, "I think I'll bake a special prune cake." Today is Christmas Eve and that is what everyone is doing, baking and cooking for the midnight dinner.

She has very few ingredients, but we are all excited at the possibility of having cake after our Christmas Eve dinner. We do not often have cake, and especially not one made by Mom, so we are delighted and looking forward to it.

We haven't got a Christmas tree or any presents to look forward to. "Better year next year," Dad says, so we resolve not to ask for anything. I know my parents feel badly about having so little money. It shows on their faces, especially my dad when he gets sad and just walks away.

I follow him outside into the barn as he sits down on a bale of hay. I sit on his knee and hug him tight and I look into his deep blue eyes and smile. I tell him, "It is going to be okay, Dad."

He smiles and hugs me back. "I am glad you are very understanding, my daughter," he says, and we go hand in hand to see the animals in the other barn.

Dad is very strict with us, but he loves us and I feel close to him, especially right now. He tells me, "Go in the house while I finish my chores with all the animals."

Wind is whistling through the cracks that we have stuffed newspaper into earlier this morning. I can still see the daylight in the corners of our front door.

A little later, Dad comes in from doing his chores and repositions the papers. "It is getting quite cold out there," he says, as he rubs his hands together to get warmer.

The potbelly stove is on and Mom is cooking something. The tasty aroma is strong throughout our one-room house. Half-frozen cow patties are flaming up together with black coal, making our room warm and smelly.

As we are about to sit down and have an early supper, we hear a knock on our door. It is Mrs. Wasnik, a neighbor from three doors over. She is all bundled up, yet shivering and half frozen as Dad guides her inside as fast as he can.

"I just want to wish your family a Merry Christmas." She tells us, "I am all alone with no family this year."

Dad says, "Come on in to get warm and stay to share a meal with us."

Last night's soup tastes great with some dry bread to dunk in it.

"Thank you, thank you for your generosity," says Mrs. Wasnik. "God bless you."

After our tea with sugar, and some of Mom's delicious cake, we sing a few Christmas carols and share stories from years gone by.

❧ ☙

Mom is upset with Dad for drinking all the time because we don't have any money. And I know she is partly right about this. My brothers and I don't have bikes like our friends, because we cannot afford them. But often, we do not have enough money for anything.

One day I am at Grandma's side of the house for tea and cookies when a delivery of curtain material comes to the door. Grandma reaches up to her closet top shelf and opens a can full of money to pay for the material. She places the can back on the shelf, and I pretend I haven't seen anything and keep eating my cookie.

The next day my brother Stan and I come from school and no one is home. Our grandparents and parents are at the farms, and two friends ride up on their bikes to go to practice for school games. When they leave, we feel really bad that we can't join them. Stan says, "John is selling his bike because he wants to get a bigger one. We could buy it for twenty dollars, but we have no money."

I tell Stan, "I know where we can get some money, but I don't know if we should."

After a long discussion, we decide to go and check out Grandma's can. "There is so much money here, she won't miss any if we borrow some," Stan says. We count out twenty dollars and put the rest back on the shelf. We run to John's place and bring the bike home.

Both of us are having fun on it when Grandma comes home and sees us on the bike.

"Whose bike is that?" she asks.

Stan answers, "Ah, it is ours now."

"Where did you get the money for it?"

"Mom gave it to us," he says. We think that since Grandma doesn't speak to Mom we are safe. And like Stan said, Grandma has lots of money in her can and she won't miss any.

For the next couple of weeks, every time I look at Grandma I feel guilty. I know she knows that we stole her money, but she doesn't say anything to us. Her actions show she doesn't trust us any longer, and she asks us to stay away from her side of the house from now on.

After a few days on the bike I tell my brother we should give the bike back to John. He reluctantly agrees and we make a plan to plead with John after school the next day. After I agree to do John's homework for a week, he gives us the money back.

After supper we go to see Grandma and confess to our crime. She looks very disappointed in us, but takes the money and tells us sternly, "Don't you ever do anything like that again, or I will report you to the authorities. You have to earn the money first before you can spend it. I am saving this money to buy another farm to make life a little easier for all of us." She puts the can away. "Now go and do your chores."

The train is jiggling back and forth, and an older man sitting a few rows from me pulls out a little paper and he pours chopped tobacco from a small pouch into it. Even this far away, I can smell the strong scent of fresh tobacco. He rolls the paper tight and licks the edge to seal it. I have seen my Grandpa Kula doing just that many times before.

Grandpa is small in stature. He wears a big hat with a large rim, a dark jacket, black pants, a plaid shirt and brown boots, and he usually has a homemade cigarette hanging out of his mouth. Most of the time his cigarette is not lit. He lights it up and few minutes later it will go out, but the butt hangs all day on his bottom lip.

Grandpa grows his own tobacco. At harvest time I help him string up the leaves and we hang them around the house to dry. When they are dry, he chops them and stores them in big coffee cans. He will enjoy his rolled cigarettes for the whole year until the next harvest. When I tell him I don't like the smell of his cigarettes, he says, "I smoke for therapeutic reasons only. They are good for me because they are organic, free of pollutants, and they are healing herbs."

Grandma walks into the house and gives Grandpa a disapproving look. Her look says clearly, "Get that stuff out of here. I hate the smell of your tobacco," even though no words come from her lips. There is a tight moment in the room with just the sound of an old grandfather clock ticking away.

"You give me heart palpitations with your nonsense," Grandpa says loudly. Grandma shakes her head and out she goes, slamming the door behind her. It is one of the few times Grandpa gets his way.

"Are you going to write about all this in your notebook as well?" Grandpa asks, smiling.

"Uh-huh," I confirm.

Grandpa is a wise and interesting man and knows a lot about natural medicine and herbs. He grows herbs in our back yard to make drops for whatever ails people. The most popular are drops for heart, liver, kidney and common colds. He is very busy, especially in the winter months, helping a lot of people as they flow in and out of the house for healings and herbal consultations, drops, or cupping against colds and flu. He speaks softly and he puts people at ease with a sweet snack and milk tea.

Coming from a family of eleven siblings, he had to make his way in life to sustain the family. They moved to a city after the first war, to get work. He practiced his therapies in the city before moving into our small town. He eats very little, mostly the vegetables and herbs from his garden.

Grandpa is always willing to help us with our homework when we are stuck. He reads lots of books and seems to know a lot about everything. He is a dramatic storyteller and shares his experiences in the war. He always starts out slowly, with lots of pauses. "Go on, what happened next?" I will ask, even if I've already heard the story before. I love listening to him and always learn something new. Through his stories, he takes me on adventures that I always dream about.

Grandma and Grandpa have a ladder to their attic, which is only accessible from their side of the house. I know he stores his old treasures there. One day Grandpa stays home while Grandma goes to their plot of land two kilometers away. He is busy behind the house in his garden and his front door is left open, so I climb the narrow ladder to his attic to see what he is hiding.

The stack of yellow, worn-out paper has a musty smell. I carefully open the folded pages, and to my surprise I find Grandpa's stories. Next to that stack is a box full of pictures with discolored and torn edges. Grandpa is standing so very handsome in his uniform. I become obsessed with his pictures and want to claim them as my own.

Grandpa does not mind that I am looking at his treasures. He gives me more than his stories to read; he gives me ideas and hope. I promise myself that I will become courageous like Grandpa, full of adventure, and do something good with my life. I will be resourceful and inspired and one day I'll be able to travel and see the world. The magical box of long-ago treasures transforms me and ignites my imagination to write more stories. I want to be just like Grandpa when I grow up.

Chapter Seventeen

❧ ❦

It is my favorite time of the year. The cherry trees are bursting with beautiful white petals. It looks like they have been reborn after lying dormant all winter, and now once again they are alive. Soon I will be able to experience the smell and the freshness of their juicy red fruit. The sky is blue, the sun is bright, and the grass is deep green. It is one of my many blessings to see this beauty. Life is less painful when I have beautiful things to look forward to.

Today Mom says, "Let's you and I walk Babunia to the pasture." Our pasture is a bit of land near the river, and nothing grows on it except for grass that later turns into hay. It is a long walk from our home, along several dirt streets and across two bridges. We bring old heavy sheets to bring back some weeds and tall grasses for the other animals to eat.

This reminds me of when Mom and I go to the river and do the laundry, and we drag the old scrub board with us. The river is about one kilometer away, but the wash smells nice and fresh on the line afterward. Because our animals walk around in the back yard, some days our clean wash ends up pulled to the ground and we have to wash it all over again. We have dirt front yards, too, and animals run around and poop just about everywhere. There is much to do here every single day, plus pull weeds on our other property farther away. Life on this farm is all-consuming.

As I am getting older, I can see my life will be no different than my parents', especially my mom's. Her main duties are cooking, cleaning, looking after children, milking the cow, making soups and pastas from scratch, hauling water from the well, cleaning barns, feeding animals, and washing clothes by hand and hanging them on the outside line to get dirty again.

These duties are fit in between working on the farm pulling weeds and carrying them home on our backs in folded sheets, for the animals to eat.

Being the oldest, I have more responsibilities than my brothers. Looking after them and keeping them busy so they don't get into trouble or accidents is a big part of my job. My quiet time is very limited and special. I take my writing paper and pencil and sit under the willow tree when I take Babunia to our pasture, practicing a medley of songs as we walk there and home again.

Sometimes when I need quiet time, Grandma lets me go into the attic. The old rocking chair and Grandpa's box of old photos keep me occupied for a while. I pretend it is my office, my private space, and no one is allowed here.

In the summer months, we take salt and bread with us each morning we go to our patch of land. We can hardly wait to enjoy our delicious fresh vegetable lunch. We plant different kinds of vegetables, but the cucumbers and tomatoes are my favorite. I check the stalks and under the leaves every day to see the flowers coming up. Next, I see the buds opening up and the small fruits showing their faces. It is a wonderful experience to plant seeds and to watch the tiny stalks push their little heads up through the brown earth, and to see them reaching upward and spreading their leaves toward the sun and their branches toward the sky. It is a miracle in itself.

It was Grandma Kula who introduced me to the unusual taste of fresh cucumbers with coarse salt. The smallest cucumbers taste the best. When they are about two inches long, I cut the cucumber in half lengthwise and pour the salt on both halves. I slide the sides up and down, rubbing them against each other until liquid forms. When I bite into the cucumber, the salty juice runs down my chin and my eyes water with excitement.

My taste buds are salivating, awaiting this same experience again as we walk the grueling eight kilometers up the hill. The early morning sun is warm on our faces. Dad has dug holes in the earth so we can hide to cool off when it gets hotter.

Today we have brought Babunia with us so she can eat the fresh weeds we pull out. She is happy to be with us and gives us milk on demand for our lunch. My mom and brothers like to drink it directly from the cow, warm and foamy, leaving a mustache on each of their faces. Dad and I don't care for warm milk, so we just suck on some wheat stalks instead.

It is a long, slow trip home in the evening with Babunia. We walk down the gravel road, with its potholes and deep grooves from wagon wheels, and sing our church songs to help pass the time. Exhausted, we feed all the animals while Mom starts some supper. After rushing to wash up for dinner, we lay down to rest until supper is ready. By then, we are fast asleep. Mom is disappointed, but she covers us with blankets and lets us sleep like that until early morning.

The next day, our pigs are happy to get the leftovers for their daily meal. They enjoy our last night's supper as we leave for the farm to repeat the same ritual as yesterday.

Nothing is more satisfying than fresh produce right from the vine. At times like this, I almost look forward to our trip to pull weeds in the scorching sun.

A gentle tap on my shoulder and Mom's soft voice wakes me up. "Do you still want to go with me to get bread?"

I open my eyes and see that it is dark outside and I cover my head.

She shakes me a bit and says, "Let's go and we'll be back soon so you can go back to sleep."

I slide out of my warm bed softly so I don't wake up my brothers. I put on my clothes and shoes and we leave quietly without waking anyone.

The town's bakery is about one kilometer down the road. We have no wood to heat our oven so it is Mom's job to get up early and buy bread before anyone wakes up. She has always gone alone, but today I am with her, keeping her company. I wanted to help her, and I also want to see if the stories regarding other people in the lineup are true.

By 3 a.m. Mom and I are standing in the long lineup. People are pushing and shoving each other to get to the front of the line. Adults are behaving like spoiled children and some of them are calling others bad names. Under the wooden steps going upstairs where the bakers live, I notice small dogs are hiding from all the yelling. I don't understand these people or why they are behaving like this, but it seems it is normal for this regular everyday ritual.

The baker and his wife are an elderly couple, and I see their tired faces as we approach closer to the front of the line. I am sure they need a break from all the screaming. "I was here first," "I have five children to feed," "I have a sick wife," "I have a sick mother," "I have to go to work soon," and on and on.

As we approach the baker, he seems to be calm and tries to divide his batch of bread fairly between the people, but some at the back of the line will definitely go home empty-handed.

Sometimes, Mom goes the night before. After she makes supper, cleans up the dishes, and puts us to bed, she walks to the bakery to wait in the lineup until it opens. Others will already be waiting. Most of the people will repeat this cycle every two days because the bakery is only open every second day and is closed on Sundays. There is no extra wood for anyone to burn in their stoves, so most people must buy their bread this way. Our baker and his wife are very nice people but they can't keep up with the demand.

Today, we receive only one loaf even though we want two—one for Grandma and Grandpa, and one for us. One loaf to share between seven people, for two days, and then Mom has to go through this nightmare all over again.

Walking home, Mom and I hold hands. She is singing Christian songs and I am humming to the tune. I look up to the sky as the sun begins to shine warm rays on us.

Chapter Eighteen

Catholicism is taught to us daily in our school, and we are being scared to death to make sure we are good. We all attend Catholicism classes regularly as part of our curriculum. Our teacher will ask many questions like, "What are the ten commandments?" If we give wrong answers, we have to see our principal. We also have to stay after school and write out the right answer one hundred times.

One day, Miss Agnes asks me, "Would you like to stop by my house after school for a glass of lemonade?" I am delighted she wants me to come over and visit with her. I say, "I will come over only for a short time, as I have chores to do when I get home."

Miss Agnes lives alone in a small house with a short yellow fence that we walk by most days after school. The inside of her house is very clean. She has never been married and has no children to mess it up. She invites me to have a seat on a soft, fluffy chair. Then she praises me for all my good work, and tells me, "I wanted to let you know that I have asked the principal to allow me to hang some of your drawings in the hallway. They are a good example for the other students in our classroom, and I think they would be a good example for the students in the entire school."

"Thank you," I say, feeling shy. "Thank you very much."

Miss Agnes is very gentle and always nice to me, giving me compliments all the time—things I never hear at home. We have our drinks and talk, mostly about my life and what I would like to do when I grow up. "You don't have to live here forever and be a farmer's wife, if that is not what you want," she says. "With your talents you can do just about anything you put your mind to."

She hugs me goodbye, and I walk home elated, feeling really good about myself and hopeful that one day I will make a difference in this world. That night I try to sleep but I am excited to think Miss Agnes might be allowed to put artwork in the school halls, and I am worried because I am thinking about our principal.

Our principal is very stern. He doesn't talk much, but when he speaks, everyone listens. He is tall with a short mustache directly under his nose and he has a very short haircut. He walks around with a strap in his right hand at all times.

He comes into our classroom often and walks between the rows of small desks, slapping his hand with the strap. "I am looking for someone who is not paying attention to the teacher," he announces, "or not doing your work like you should." Everyone pays attention when the principal is in the room. Some kids say he will give the strap to anyone just to see himself in control. I have never had to talk to the principal, and that is the way I want it to stay. Finally, I drift off to sleep.

I am a good student and keep my nose in my books. But one morning the principal calls for me. "See me in my office later today, after the classes are over."

This is the most frightening day of my life. I know I didn't do anything wrong, but we never know with the principal's moods. I can't even eat my lunch and I have an upset stomach. I feel like throwing up. The last class finally ends and my homeroom teacher reminds me, "Don't forget to see the principal before you go home."

I keep reminding myself that I am a good student, always getting 100 per cent on all my tests. I even do an extra few pages after I finish my homework so I know what the teacher is talking about the next day. I am shaking as I open the principal's door.

His office is narrow and long and he is sitting by his large desk, at the very end. "Come on in, child," he motions, as I approach him slowly. "Don't be nervous or scared, I am not going to hurt you. I asked to see you because your drawings and paintings are quite nice, and you capture the trees, fruits, birds, and the animals really well."

"Thank you, sir," I muster.

I am still confused as to why I am here. I had not expected to be called to talk to him about my artwork. But we do not interrupt our principal. I know that for sure, as I witnessed John, a boy in my class, getting a strap last week for interrupting him.

"Your paintings are very well done and I want to use them as an example for other students."

"Thank you, sir," I say again.

He scratches his mustache, and with an unusually soft voice he asks me, "May I have your permission to hang your pictures in all the halls, please?"

I am speechless with surprise, but inside I am feeling delighted with pride.

"I wanted to be sure you didn't mind. Well, what do you say, may we hang them up tomorrow?" He smiles at me.

I nod yes and smile back at him.

Our principal has had the reputation of a monster, but for the first time, I see him as a human being, with the same feelings as the rest of us.

I run home as fast as I can to tell my parents the good news. Mom looks up from her work and says, "You are late," so I keep quiet until I finish my chores.

Later, I explain enthusiastically, "I was asked for permission by the principal to hang my pictures on the school walls."

"More work and less playing around would be much better," Mom says.

"Now, now, leave the girl alone," says Dad. "Let her have a moment of enjoyment for her accomplishments."

After supper, Dad and I sit down and draw a few more pictures. I keep thinking that art is just not my mom's interest, as I go to bed content with this day.

After that, Miss Agnes often invites me for tea after school and shows me her books and pictures. I love her, and she says often that she loves me, too. With no children of her own she feels close to me and wants to teach me anything I want to learn. I am so very blessed to know her.

On Tuesday we have a math exam. I am happy because it is my favorite subject and I am pretty sure I will get my usual 100 per cent. My math teacher, Mr. Wolchek, is a young man, newly married and very sure of himself. He marks all the papers and hands them back to us. When I receive mine, he winks at me with a smile. For sure I have a perfect mark, I think, smiling back at him.

I am walking home when I open my paper. On the top in red pen it says, "Good job." Underneath it says "98%." I sit on the side of the road scanning my test for a mistake but cannot find it.

All the way home I am crying. My dad will be very disappointed in me for not being the best. "You have to be Number One at everything you do," he often says. "Number Two is a loser."

After supper, he brings it up. "How did you do on your exam today," he says with a smile, "or should I even ask?"

Gloom comes over me. I have my head down on that paper and can't find the mistake.

"Let me see what you are staring at all this time," he says, reaching for it. "Ninety-eight! What happened, where did you go wrong? Is studying with your girlfriend making you not concentrate on your work?"

"No, Dad," I say. "I have been over this paper many times and I can't find the mistake. Please, can you double check it and see where I am wrong?"

He looks it over for a while. "I cannot find the mistake either," he says. I go to bed confused.

The next day at school I approach Mr. Wolchek and ask if he could look over my paper again. He curls up his nose and tells me to get back to my seat. "I don't have time for any of that nonsense," he says. "My markings are final."

After school, I run to Miss Agnes's home and show her my paper. She looks at it reluctantly and scans it over a few times. "There are no mistakes that I see on this paper. I will talk to Mr. Wolchek tomorrow."

The next day, Mr. Wolchek is angry that I went behind his back to another teacher and complained about his marking. But he concedes, "I will take a closer look at your test paper later."

When I get back to the classroom my paper says "100%" in big red writing and a note at the bottom says, "I don't usually give a perfect mark to anyone, because students will not try hard enough to study for their tests." I will always try hard, because I will never be satisfied with less than 100 per cent.

༄ ༅

After Mom's parents went to Canada, Mom was glad she lived close to all her aunts and uncles. Uncle Fred and Aunt Mary, as we call them, are very old. It is convenient to visit with them as they now live across the street from us. They are poor and sickly but they have big smiles on their faces when we show up.

Their house is on a small piece of land, and they grow all their vegetables in their back yard. They are both elderly but they are determined to not be a burden on our family. They are always positive and uplifting, even though their only daughter, Constance, ran away to a big city years ago to get married. They don't see her often, but they look at her picture and dream that one day she will come back.

Their health is failing and they are sick a lot. The small one-room house is filled with an old table and two chairs and it has one window. It has a potbelly stove to keep them warm in the winter and a small stove to cook on. They have one small bed and an old dresser in one corner. The paint is peeling off the walls everywhere, but the house is warm and cozy.

Uncle Fred is the oldest of the seven kids. My Grandpa Janiga, who lives in Canada, is his younger brother. I like Uncle Fred. He always stops to talk to me and asks me, "How is the prettiest girl I know doing today?"

I say, "She is doing just fine," and he nods and goes about his business with his chickens and his pig.

Auntie Mary bakes bread occasionally, and the smell comes all the way to our front yard. I run over to investigate what she is baking, and I always help her with something and get a good treat. Auntie's baking tastes very good, and I tell her so. Often she calls me for my approval of different things she bakes.

Today, I brought one of my story books and read to them both. I know they miss their daughter by the way they look at her picture. They only have two pictures of her. One is from when she was very little and the other is from when she got married. Not many people in our town have cameras, so not many of us have pictures.

Auntie Mary likes me and asks me to come and visit often. She gets sick a lot, mostly in the winter, and spends her days in bed. I bring her a jar of cherries, an apple, or a glass of milk, and read to her.

When Uncle Fred gets sick also, we don't see anyone come out of their house for days. I am always afraid that one day they may both die and no one will know.

It is a sad day today for Uncle Fred, as we have buried Auntie Mary. He is lost without her and doesn't know what to do. Their daughter is saying her goodbyes and leaving on the train this afternoon to return to her life in the big city. I feel sorry for my uncle, but Dad says, "This is real life and we have to accept God's decision to take good people to his kingdom."

I try to visit Uncle Fred often. He sits in his chair, staring at a picture from his wedding and wishing Aunt Mary was still alive. I sit with him a while, just holding his hand. As I am leaving I say, "I promise to come back soon."

Some days we visit and don't say much, and some days we talk about his chickens he loves so much and why he is always feeding them. "I will never forget you, Uncle Fred," I tell him.

He still greets me with, "How is the prettiest girl I know, today?" I love hearing those words from him, as no one else says them to me like he does and means it. I will miss Uncle Fred when he is gone.

Chapter Nineteen

Hide-and-go-seek is one of our favorite games. One person puts their hands over their eyes and counts to ten, and the rest of us run and hide in all different places. After the counting stops, that person tries to find us.

On this sunny day we are running in our back yard through the orchard. I decide to run past my brother and two friends all the way to the back edge of our property.

To my horror, I find our dog, Teddy, lying lifeless in the shallow ditch. I pick up a small stick and poke at him, but he doesn't move. The others are afraid to touch the dog and they run home.

I run home as fast as I can to tell my dad what I have found. Out of breath I shout, "Our dog is dead, our dog is dead."

Dad is cleaning the shed. "Slow down and get your breath," he says. "What happened and where is Teddy?"

As I am explaining what I have seen, my dad is getting angrier by the minute. "I knew something like this must have happened to our dog when he was missing early this morning." He starts swearing about our neighbor as we run to the orchard. "That no-good-for-nothing Mr. Tan poisoned our dog. I just feel it in my bones."

"Why do you think our neighbor killed Teddy?" I ask.

"Mr. Tan threatened to get rid of him about a hundred times when he was barking," says Dad.

It was true that Teddy barked often, but that was because people kept using our yard for a shortcut. He was just protecting our yard.

Dad carries Teddy's lifeless body home and he puts the dog on the big bench outside the barn. "Oh my God," he yells, "I can smell kielbasa on the dog's breath and I see a couple of pieces of crushed glass in his mouth. Mr. Tan did kill our dog. Most likely he lured the dog to the orchard and gave him some kielbasa mixed with glass pieces from a soda bottle."

Dad is upset with our neighbor and he is devastated about the death of our watchdog. He loves all the animals and doesn't want any harm to come to them. His face is getting very red. "I am going to tear Mr. Tan apart with my bare hands when I get hold of him."

Dad can have a real bad temper, but I have never seen him this angry before and he sounds like he means it. Whenever he gets angry at my mom, I try to get him to go for a walk with me to calm him down. But this time I am searching for the right words to say and none of them are working. He is beating his fists on the bench. I see his knuckles bleeding, but Dad doesn't even notice.

I run in the house to get a rag for Dads' bleeding hand and a glass of water to calm him. He looks at me very angrily, but he takes the glass from me and gulps the water down. "Here," he says as he passes the empty glass back to me. "Now you are happy?"

I start to cry and hug my dad. "I know you miss Teddy and so do I." Some people make fun of my dad for caring about his animals so much, and they call him all kinds of nicknames relating to animals. I know that Dad does not like those names and tries to ignore them.

After a long embrace, I convince him to bury Teddy in the back orchard under the apple tree, close to where I found him. We get the shovel and go to dig a big hole.

Sweat is pouring off Dad's forehead as he digs in the dry dirt, and I am asking God to accept our dog into his kingdom. "Thank you, Jesus."

"Amen," Dad says, as we lower our dog's body into the deep hole. On our walk back to the house, I try to remember all the funny, smart things our dog did. "I remember when Teddy stood on his back legs only, wiggling his tail in a funny way and sort of counting with his bark. Remember when you taught him to play different games? Teddy was able to learn them quickly."

"He was a good dog," Dad says. "I will miss him. Well, we better get back to our chores before the day disappears." But he looks toward Mr. Tan's house and tells me, "This is not over. When Mr. Tan gets home from the farm I will be dealing with him appropriately."

I look up at him and say, "That is what I am afraid of, Dad."

Dad has that look again, and he almost smiles and walks away.

I walk toward the house praying, "God, please resolve this conflict and let there be peace between us and Mr. Tan."

After supper we all pray for Teddy.

The next morning the sun is shining through our windows and I hear voices coming from the outside. Mr. Tan and Dad are shouting at each other. Mr. Tan denies that he is responsible for the death of our dog.

"I don't believe you," my dad keeps saying.

I walk over and take Dad's hand and say, "Let's go for a walk." Dad looks at me and nods as we walk away.

We talk more about Teddy and how we all loved him and how much we will miss him. Dad reminds me, "We are going to the Jarmark tomorrow and I will buy you something nice. Thank you for being a good girl."

After a while, another dog joins our barnyard family. But it is many months before my Dad stops being so angry with Mr. Tan.

In the fall, Dad and Mom gather extra vegetables, grain, and some of our birds and animals, and we all go to sell them on the open market. We usually make a few dollars for the necessary things that we don't grow on our farm. Today Dad promises me, "I will buy you new shoes if we make extra money and maybe a small doll for being a good girl with all your help."

The day is long and boring. I smile at the passersby that touch all the vegetables and ask for cheaper prices. Mom and Dad look exhausted from serving people since early morning. Finally they start to pack things up to go home.

The late afternoon sun is still hot and we are all thirsty. I walk down the row to one of the merchants who had lots of water earlier. His water is now all gone and he tells me, "Go to the house around the corner and an elderly lady who lives there will give you some water."

Sweat is pouring off my forehead as I walk toward her place, but finally I am at her front door. "Knock, knock," I say.

"Who's there?" a deep voice answers.

"A girl with a plastic jug to get some drinking water," I say.

"Come on in," is the invitation, so I push the door open and go inside. Two men are sitting at the table drinking, and it looks like they are having some kind of whiskey, similar to what my dad drinks. They are laughing and pointing at me, and I feel very uncomfortable.

"May I have some drinking water, please?" I ask politely.

"Yes, you may," the older, unshaven man answers. "Come closer so we can fill up your jug."

Slowly I venture to the big pail full of water sitting on the floor, and I lower my jug to fill it to the top. "Thank you so much," I mutter and proceed to the front door.

The second man stands up and puts his arm on the door and says, "Now that we have given you the water, we need a payment in return."

"I don't have any money to give you," I say.

"Well, well," the older man chants, "what are you going to give us in exchange for this delicious water?"

"I have an old doll at our selling spot. I will go and get it and bring it right back for you."

"We don't need any old doll," he says, "so I guess you can stay here and clean for us all week to pay off your debt. Your parents can get you next week when they come back to the market."

My heart is pounding very fast and I am looking around for some kind of distraction so I can run outside. At this point there is a knock on the door, and when the man opens it a tall young man asks for water. I dash out quickly between them.

The spot where my parents were is cleaned up and they are nowhere to be found. What am I going to do? Our wagon is gone and I don't know where to look for it. Most of the people have already left and the remaining few are packed up and leaving.

I feel so lost, abandoned, and not wanted. Why did they not wait for me? Don't they even know that I am missing? Are they looking for me? I am terrified; those two men are going to find me here and I will never see my family again. I sit on a rock crying and praying for God to send my parents back to pick me up. "Please God, help me to be safe."

Why did I go looking for water without telling anyone? Then I hear a horse coming and I see Dad and Mom waving their arms. Thank you, God, I am safe. The new shoes or the new doll will have to wait for another time. For now, I am glad I am going home, no matter what the punishment will be.

Chapter Twenty

My dad is an only child, but he has lots of cousins and most of them are very close to him, almost like brothers. Uncle Edward is one of his closest cousins and a great friend, and they often work together when more adults are needed for a job.

Coming home from school, I see Uncle Edward is in our hay barn with my dad. I wave hello, then go into the house and have a glass of milk and give some to my brothers. The boys go outside to play and I proceed to do my homework. I am very involved with my math, solving another difficult problem, when all of a sudden I hear our pig, Dusia, squeal.

Dad gave our pig her name. She looks Dad right in the eye most of the time, and she thinks she is human. Dad says, "She knows what I am thinking, and goes into her stall without a fight." She likes it when we bring her fresh leaves and the fruit that falls from our fruit trees for her dinner. Most days, Mom cooks the peelings from our vegetables for Dusia, and some days she eats our dinner leftovers as well. She is a happy pig, and she likes it here.

Now, it sounds like she is crying. I look through the window and I see her lying on the floor of the barn. I close my eyes. I don't want to think about what is happening to our pig.

One of the jobs Uncle Edward and Dad do together is the necessary job of killing animals for food and sharing the meat. We have no refrigeration systems, so they smoke most of our meat to preserve it for the winter.

The squealing does not stop. I jump up from my seat and run outside to see what is happening. By this time, I see Dusia hanging upside down from the rafters in the barn, wiggling and crying. I yell at my dad to stop hurting her, but he orders me to get in the house and do my homework.

I am very upset and slam the door behind me, but I can still hear squealing coming from the pig. With my face covered and crying uncontrollably, I realize this must be the way to kill pigs so we can have some meat to eat.

After the squealing has stopped, I look through the window and the pig is not moving. Uncle Ed is cutting her tummy open from her head to her back end. Stuff is falling out of the pig's tummy and Dad is putting it in the pail. Our chickens and ducks walk around. They are picking at their favorite food like worms, bugs and spilled grain. They have no idea they might be our next meal. I sob while I am finishing my homework, and I promise myself I will not eat our pet pig.

After they finish with the pig, Dad tries to explain to me why they have to kill it that way and why we kill our animals in the first place. He reminds me, "That is why we raise our birds and animals, so we can have food to eat."

I tell him, "I am not touching that meat ever," and he smiles and says, "Not until you get hungry and then you will eat it." But meat has never appealed to me, though I do force myself on some occasions to eat small portions.

Later, I am playing in the barn, jumping on the big bales of hay and straw with my brother. The scene of the killing of our pig is still very vivid to me and will echo through my mind forever. I remember how Dusia squealed and cried for her life, and I was not able do anything to stop it. Where was I the last time Dad and Uncle Ed did that procedure? I'd rather not know when they are killing the next animal. I will make sure I will not be home to witness it.

The rolling hills around our town are very picturesque with lots of green trees. Farms, small houses, outbuildings and barns make up our community. The dirt road behind our homestead is rough, full of potholes and has a big steep hill to climb, so wagons do not use it. We walk this road summer and winter to school, as it is much shorter than our main paved road, and it is a shortcut when we walk to our farm so far away.

On one side of this narrow dirt road there is a steep hill, and on the other are orchards full of cherry and apple trees that grow right up to the edge of the road. At dusk the hill brings shadows, and the trees sway and make strange sounds as if they are talking to each other. We are always in fear that someone is hiding in the orchard on that stretch of the road and will scare us when we pass by. We have no vehicles in our town, but we always expect to come in contact with someone walking at all hours of the day and night.

My Auntie Kazia lives on that road, a little more than a kilometer from us. We pass her house every day as we walk to school. One day after school I stop by her place to pull weeds with my cousin, Jany. They have a big garden behind their house, and the best time to pull weeds is after it rains like it did last night. We laugh while we work.

After supper, we are doing some homework when we realize it is getting dark much sooner than normal. My auntie looks outside and says, "We will have more rain tonight." I need to get home fast before total dark is upon us. Jany walks with me halfway, then I must walk the rest of the way by myself.

A breeze blows across the road, lifting the dirt and twirling it around like a cocoon. I approach our neighbor's long orchard and the trees start whispering to me. The sound is eerie and my heart is pumping really fast. It feels like it is going to jump right out of my chest. I think about Uncle Edward, who recently had a heart attack. My dad says that Uncle Edward's heart was jumping too fast when he met a large dog walking at night on this road last month, and it caused him to be very ill.

I keep repeating my daily prayer, "Be with me, Lord, always, and especially now." I walk past this orchard very slowly and keep my eyes on the road ahead. Only a few more minutes and I will be safe on our property.

Right now the clouds are dark and heavy. In the distance I see a big tall shadow coming toward me. I hope it is only a neighbor walking home. I continue to pray, "Lord, please comfort me." I am shaking in my boots, but I tell myself, "I am nine years old now and the Lord is walking with me. I am not afraid of anything or anyone."

As I approach the tall man, he speaks. "I am so glad you are alright, my girl, we were worried about you when you didn't get home before dark." My dad, my hero, has come to rescue me. Trembling, I run into his arms. I don't say a word, and I will not let go of him.

Dad is angry with me, but I don't get a spanking from him. Mom is another story. She says, "That kind of behavior should be rewarded with a spanking, for sure."

Then she tells me, "You scared us half to death. Besides the rumbling trees at night on that narrow dark road, there are different people who live in the houses around the orchards. They keep to themselves for a reason, and most people are afraid of them. The first house has a big dog that barks very loudly and runs around loose at night. The second house has a challenged man who wanders all the time through the orchards. The third house has two young girls who are locked up when their parents are not at home, and a strange smell comes out of that house. The fourth house on the left side of the road is a large homestead with many small buildings around the house. No one knows how many families live in that house. They all look very different and scary, and most of them have no teeth."

I promise my parents I will not come home this late ever again, and I surely will keep my promise.

After that lecture from Mom, Dad gives me that "look" and he doesn't say another word to me. I have lots to think about now. I am still trembling because of being afraid in the dark, but I am also trembling as I think of how I have disappointed my parents.

Now I know who lives around us and I will be very careful walking by myself at night. I go to bed right after supper thinking about what could have happened if Dad had not rescued me.

Chapter Twenty-One

Going through deep and muddy holes in the road to our land each day is hard on the wagon, and often we find Dad fixing the wagon wheels as they are always missing spokes.

Our wagon is a rectangle three meters long and one meter wide. Nailed high above the sides is the bench we sit on and a brake handle on the right side. It is our only transportation to the fields. With one loaf of bread and two buckets of water we are set for the hot day.

Sometimes, big ruts in the dirt road shake the buckets of water and spill half of it. When we get to the field Dad tells us, "The horse needs water more than we do, as he has to take us home at night." It is hard work in the hot sun all day without much water to drink.

Last week after the rain, the wagon got stuck in a mud hole and our horse couldn't pull us out. We were about five kilometers from the farm land and frightened that we would be stuck there for the day. After trying to get out for what seemed like hours, Dad got off the wagon and whispered something into the horse's ear. The horse looked at us sitting there and all at once it took off and pulled the wagon out of the hole. I'm not sure what the message to the horse was, but the horse got much stronger. Later Dad said, "It is our secret what I said to the horse."

Dad painted the wagon's side boards green and the wheel spokes bright red. "It looks like a Christmas tree coming down the road," I told him.

"I like bright colors and I won't change it," Dad replied. Many times we plead with him to change the color, as the townspeople sometimes point at us and laugh, but Dad will say, "Oh, come on, this is not the end of the world, this color will do fine."

అ ఆ

Today is Saturday, and it is going to be a scorcher. I wake up Mom by shaking her arm. "Get up, we have to water all the animals and put them in the barn for the day. We have to get to the farm before it is too hot. Dad is hitching the horse to the wagon and calling for us."

Mom mumbles something as I am getting my brothers ready to go. "I don't feel so good today," she finally says. I help her to get up and dressed.

I climb into the wagon with my hair uncombed and join my brothers. Mom hands us each a piece of dry bread and a cup of cold water for on the way. "This will keep you until lunch," she says, as Dad is yelling, "Let's get going now."

Driving in this heat, I feel like we might roast alive if we keep going. Our horse is walking slowly, snorting and foaming all over. Sweat is pouring off his back, and he keeps turning around to look at us in the wagon like we are crazy for travelling in this heat, as if to say, "I want to go back home."

Sweat is running down my chest and soaking the elastic band in my panties. I look at Dad. "Let us go back home before we cook," I say.

"We need to keep going," says Dad. "The ground is still soft for a few more hours after last night's rain, but it will dry up quickly." I know it is much harder to pull weeds when the ground is hard, but it is too hot to work. No one listens to me. I am only a kid.

I like to take mental vacations, going somewhere peaceful and relaxing even when things around me are not peaceful or relaxing. At night I lie on my sleeping blanket behind the tall dresser and dream about another lifetime. I fall asleep listening to my parents arguing about money and how much they don't have. I know that we have no money for anything extra. We barely survive from one day to the next.

I repeat to myself over and over, "When I grow up, I will work at any job so as not to be broke. I want to see the world and learn different languages and do many different things. I will always have money for everything I need."

When I tell my mom my plans for my future, she says, "Sure you will," and keeps doing what she is doing. I don't think she even hears what I say. I have no one in my family to talk to or share my dreams with.

Mom hums every day as she works. She says, "It helps me not to think about anything that is going on in our lives." I don't want to think about it either, how broke we are and how Dad and Mom fight all the time. I want to explore the world and be more than we are on our small farm in this little farming community. We have no television, only a small radio that works part of the time when Dad gives it a good hit with his hand. We accept what is told to us by our dad. When he speaks, we listen, as no one wants to get the strap for not paying attention. But there has to be more out there in this big world than what I see here.

Finally we arrive at the farm, climb down from the wagon, and get to work. Pulling weeds is always a sweaty job. Every twenty minutes, we hide under the wagon from the scorching sun.

After we run out of water, Dad finally announces, "Gather all the stuff. It is a little too hot to be here today, and we have lots of chores to get done at home."

Mom doesn't say anything, just nods and gathers the weeds we pulled for the animals back home.

Later that day, I hear a noise above my head, and when I look up I see a small plane. I wonder where it is going and how it can hold people up in the air, being so small. I run to tell my mom to look up and see the plane. She looks up from feeding chickens, and says, "My daddy, your Grandpa Janiga, is coming for me. He will take me to his place in Canada and I won't have to work so hard anymore."

I look sadly at my Mom. "I don't like that plane. It is going to take you away from us and we won't have our Mom once again."

She pats my back and assures me, "If I go, I will take you and the whole family with me. Don't worry, my daughter, the Lord will work things out for us."

Perhaps I've been a little too proud showing off my new purse. I told my brother Stan I could ride the bike and take my purse with me. I did, and that was the last time I saw it.

"I am sure someone has found it and will return it very soon," he says. We retrace our steps to no avail and all evening I stew about it. I toss and turn all night thinking about what will happen if no one finds it. All my notes will be lost. "What if they read my notes?" I pray, "Lord, give me peace about this."

The next morning it is very hard to concentrate on anything other than my carelessness and the loss of my purse. Yesterday, Grandma K. gave me three dollars for helping with her chores and I forgot to hide it with the rest of the money. It is still in my purse. I am praying out loud, "God, use me and my lost purse with the few dollars in it in any way You want to. In Jesus's name, Amen."

An instant peace comes over me and I know that I will see my purse again.

Finally, evening comes. I am all alone and trying to do my homework when knock on our front door startles me. I open the door and see a neighbor from down the road, carrying my purse. "I thought it might be important to you," she says. "I found it in some thick grass when I was walking my dog earlier. He was sniffing something near it."

"Thank you, thank you, I am most grateful that you've found it," I tell her. But if she read my notes, I am in big trouble. "How did you know it was mine?"

"I unzipped the pocket and saw the notebook with your name on it, and thought it might be homework," she says. "I hope you'll find all your treasures are still in there."

I thank her again a few more times and say, "God bless you for your honesty."

All my writings are in my bag and the money is still there. Everything around me is much brighter and I am very happy.

Not long after I got my purse back, Auntie Veronica arrives in Topola from the big city for a short visit. She is here to cheer my mom. Mom has been very sad and not feeling well. Some days she doesn't want to eat or get out of bed. She only cries. She has been this way often, ever since baby Mark died many months ago.

It is nice listening to Auntie Veronica talk about her life in the big city. It sounds so much easier, and everyone seems much happier there. She fills us up with many stories about where and how they live. She tells me I have great potential to be more than a farmer, and an idea is born in my head.

I want to go to Auntie Veronica's place. I even ask her, "Can I come with you, please?"

She looks at me with her smiling eyes and sits me down on our outside bench and hugs me tight. She says, "You need to stay with your family. They need you, your mom needs you," and she hugs me again.

I feel loved and at peace just for this short instant. Finally, I let go of our embrace with tears in my eyes.

Auntie Veronica scribbles something on a piece of paper and puts it in my pocket. "This is our address," she whispers. "You can write to me and your cousin Ala anytime you wish."

"I will, I will. I promise. But how do I get to your place from the train station? Is it a long walk to your house?"

Auntie Veronica smiles and takes the paper from my pocket and draws a line with a couple of funny curves. "We go up the hill from the train station all the way to our house," she says. "When you are grown up, if you ever decide to come and visit us, it is very easy to find me and my family."

"I will come to visit one day," I promise.

Sitting with Auntie Veronica on the wooden bench under our big cherry tree with singing birds around us is the best. From this moment, I will be dreaming of better things to come.

Grandma is calling us for lunch. Auntie Veronica is going to visit her other relatives before she takes the train to return home. While we are eating, Auntie shares a few more stories of her life before we say our final goodbyes. With tears in my eyes, I confirm, "I will see you soon, Auntie Veronica."

Now that winter is coming I have a lot of things to think about.

Chapter Twenty-Two

A few weeks ago I started helping Ania, our local seamstress, with some sewing. She lives two doors over from my cousin Jana. I go to visit Jana whenever possible and sneak to Ania's place just to watch her sew.

I offer to help Ania with sweeping her floor, hemming the slacks or skirts, sewing a few buttons on blouses or dresses, or attaching collars and cuffs. I do these things for free and she is starting to trust me with more. When she notices I am doing a good job, she decides to pay me a few pennies each time I help.

Many times I tell my parents I am going to my girlfriend Halinka's place to study. But since I am my teacher's favorite girl, I don't have to study much. My teacher always helps me to understand things much easier. So I sneak to Ania's place instead, to learn more about sewing and to earn a few pennies. She shows me how to sew from clients' measurements without patterns. I love watching Ania take a big chunk of material and create a beautiful dress, skirt or blouse with lacy trims.

Ania is constantly encouraging me to become a seamstress when I grow up. She tells me I have a lot of talent for sewing and creating things with my hands. I know my parents don't want me to go over to Ania's place because they think it is a waste of time, but I long to be there and create.

Rainy weather gives me an opportunity to sneak out to see Ania because there is not much work outside. I miss playing with friends, but I have a goal: to learn how to sew and make some money. The pennies add up and I bury them in Grandpa's tobacco can under the cherry tree. Sometimes I worry that my brothers will see me hide it and tell my parents.

Sunday after church is usually a good time for me to sneak out to Ania's. We have extra company and the adults are busy visiting. I still fear that my mom will somehow find out where I go, and she will come to take me home. I can almost hear her saying, "Sunday is God's day, created for rest and prayer, not for this kind of work."

After church, company starts to arrive for a visit and I sneak outside to the outhouse. I peek through the moon-shaped hole to make sure no one is coming and I take off like a bullet to Ania's place.

Ania has a big project to finish: dresses for a coming wedding. The work is very important and I feel honored when she asks me to stay late. Now the sun has gone down behind the tall trees and the night is approaching fast. The full moon helps to light up the road except for the long dark shadows that are following me.

Water is making a thunderous noise as I cross the bridge. I can hear the townsfolk saying, "We have a big monster living under the bridge and he comes out in the dark and roars." I say a prayer and run across that bridge as fast as I can.

I still hear the water gurgling in the distance, but I have different things to worry about when I get home.

The shadows play tricks, making me think someone is following me. I run as fast as I can. I keep turning around to see who is behind me, and I trip over a stone and fall.

Looking at my scraped knee bleeding on my nice dress, I start to cry. I am calling for my mom, but she is not around. I close my eyes and pray for God to help me stay safe and to walk with me.

At that very moment I feel two arms lifting me up to safety. When I open my eyes I see it is our neighbor, Bob, who lives a few doors down from us. "Are you alright?"

"Uh-huh," I muster.

Bob is handicapped. He is an older man like my dad, and he stays home most of the time. The townspeople make fun of him and some are scared of him. But he is very kind to me. He came out of his house when he heard me cry and call for my mom.

Bob walks me to my gate. "Will you be alright for now? I don't want your dad to see me, so I better go."

"Thank you again for your help." I wave goodbye.

I walk up the steep driveway, and I keep telling myself I am not scared of the dark shadows. Next time I will be home before it gets dark—that is, if there is a next time.

Last week Mom got a promise from Ania to make a nice dress for my tenth birthday. Today, new materials have arrived at our general store and most of the people are waiting to get a look at these new prints.

I wait patiently with my mom in a long line as the storekeeper lets in five ladies at a time. As I watch the procession of ladies leaving with different pieces of colorful material, I worry there won't be any left for me. Polka dots are in style this year, my cousin Jana says, and most likely they have been sold out by now.

Three hours later, we get our chance to peruse the leftover materials, but there are none that I like. My cousin Jana left really early with a nice piece of fabric, beautiful black polka dots on a white background. She had bought enough material for dresses for her and Ania, who is her best friend. The store now has only some dark colors suited for Grandma, so Mom and I leave disappointed.

Today I am picking gooseberries behind the barn. I bite into one but it is sour and leaves a bad taste in my mouth. I keep picking them, with the idea that I will leave them to dry in the sun on my blanket. I will make a necklace and bracelet later, like the popcorn strings we make for our Christmas tree. I want to learn how to do everything. My cousin Jana was wearing a necklace and bracelet last week, but they were shiny like they were made of glass. Her mom and dad have more money, so she is always wearing something new.

Jana's mom, my grandma's sister, is visiting Grandma and they are talking about all the nice material that came to town. When I overhear them, I come to join in their conversation. I say, "I had an opportunity yesterday to get some black polka dot on white background, but it was sold out before we got inside the store." Auntie Ginny changes the topic. Disappointed, I leave to feed the animals.

Later in the afternoon, I walk to Ania's place to help with some sewing. I have been thinking for the past month about some material Ania has. It would make a gorgeous dress for the summer to wear to church, but I don't say anything about this to Ania. Now she wants to measure me up and says, "I want to keep the measurements on file for the future."

The following week when I get to Ania's place, a small black-on-white polka dot dress is hanging on a dress form and needs to be adjusted and hemmed up. I feel like a knife is cutting through me. Then Jana comes over to see me. We are laughing and teasing but the joke is mostly on me. She finally says, "I got just a smidge extra material, and between leftovers from our dresses, it was enough to make one for you."

I look at her in disbelief and say, "I will work off any chores you both need to have done." I feel privileged to have the same color dress as Jana and seamstress Ania, who are a few years older than me.

I watch my dad as he loads up our big wagon full of white beets. The wooden sides are high so no beets can escape on their journey to the sugar factory. Dad looks tired but smiles at me and says, "Let's get going. We have a long trip ahead of us. Sit beside me and hang on." We navigate through the potholes in our lower driveway. "This will be a new experience for you," he smiles.

I nod. "I will write all about it for my school project."

Kazmierza Wielka is 20 kilometers away, but our horse is used to going long distances. We talk about my school work, and Dad asks, "Are you happy, my daughter?"

I tell him, "I love school, and some kids do notice my drawings that are hanging on the walls."

"But are you happy, my girl?"

Deep inside I am dying to tell him I am not happy, that I want to live in a big city and that I don't want to be a farmer anymore. My dad was born in the big city and went to school there. He is well educated, and he often thinks about the choices that were taken away from him when he was a teenager, during World War II, and his parents took him to live in a farming town.

Does he miss city life? Does he wonder why he settled on being a farmer? For many years now he has been a farmer, so what can he do?

I don't think Dad wants to talk about city life, though, and I don't know how to answer his question. Finally I say, "I am happy I get to go on this trip with my dad."

We talk and eat our bacon-grease sandwiches that Mom made for us. I have never seen my dad this happy, relaxed, and carefree. The trip to the factory goes quickly, and soon we are back home.

Chapter Twenty-Three

Oh, Christmas, the excitement we feel for days ahead. I am inside doing my homework when I see a few flakes drift down outside the window. It is our first snowfall of the winter. We love playing in the snow, but some winters we only get rain.

The glistening snow gently falls on everything, covering the dirty ground. I quickly finish my assignments and dress warmly, then out the door I go to inspect the flakes. They are all beautiful, and each one is the size of a penny, fluffy and moist. I catch them on my tongue and they quickly disappear. I watch all the different designs as they land on my coat and boots. They look so pure and white.

I call my brother Stan. "Come out and play with me. We will make angels with our arms and legs and throw snowballs at the cherry tree."

"I can throw a lot farther," Stan says.

"I can throw a lot higher," I respond.

A call from Mom for supper interrupts our competition. The score is even and I only need one more to be a winner. I trip and fall and my brother hits the tree. "Well, now we know who is the best at throwing snowballs," he says, and walks away smiling. I pick myself up and brush off all the snow and think that tomorrow is another day and I will be more prepared.

I watch from the table as the snowflakes dance in the air, twirling around before they land. As evening approaches, the snowflakes get even bigger. "We'll have lots of snow tomorrow to finish our competition." I smile.

Christmas is approaching and we have no Christmas tree. With five of us to feed and clothe, what money we have always goes for the necessities and Dad's drinking. Mom always tries to make the best of what we have, but there is not enough for anything extra. No new clothes for us like some kids get every year.

On Christmas Eve morning, after I complain enough about not having a Christmas tree, Dad takes me to the outskirts of town where we pick up a scruffy pine. We drag it all the way home.

What about decorations?

Dad says, "Remember the year we made garlands out of strips cut out of catalogues and glued together? We do not have any catalogues right now, so why don't you kids sit down and color some pages in different colors, and then cut them into strips to make garlands?"

We make the strips about one inch wide and five inches long. Then we glue the first strip into a circle, and loop the next strips into that one before gluing it. We add more strips, one at a time, to make a long chain.

We are busy for hours making colorful garlands until the tree is full. Daddy says, "A tree fit for a king, and you were worried how it would look."

Mom has cooked all day so we can have a celebration feast of different things after Midnight Mass. Now she tells us to stop with the decorations. We have to leave right away to be at the church by midnight.

Everyone bundles up and on the road we go. To make the long walk go faster, Mom and Dad tell us stories about baby Jesus. He was very poor like us and became the King of the world. All of the townsfolk are marching along the road, singing and laughing. This is a special time of the year when everyone is extra nice and somewhat happy.

The walk home is fun. All the kids from town chase each other and play hide-and-go-seek behind the black, shadowy trees. I can hardly wait to get home to see what will magically appear on our Christmas tree. Every year when we get home from Midnight Mass, we notice some candies hanging along with our art work. We eat our late supper fast and get to our candies.

I wonder where the candies came from this year. Deep down I know that Grandma Kula had something to do with that. Last year I got a small doll. She looked like she had been loved by someone else first. I didn't care. I took good care of her and kept her always by my side. Grandma denied that she was responsible for the doll. But the next morning I found a pink ribbon on Grandma's table that matched the one in my doll's brown hair.

In my sad times, I pull out my hand-me-down doll and talk to her. "How have you been, my lovely Malgosia?" I pretend I am her mom and say, "Mommy has been very busy, but I have not forgotten about you. I love you very much. You know how much Mommy loves you, of course you do. I love you more than any little girl in the whole wide world. More than any one person could love."

Sometimes I stroke her sandy brown hair and say, "If anything goes wrong and you feel like crying for some reason, you know I will always be here to put my arms around you, hold you, and protect you. I will read you a beautiful story which is about a good little girl that nobody loves. Can you imagine anything so silly?"

Grandma Kula is always extra nice to me, more than to my brothers. She tells me often, "You need a real mother who can teach you things." I think about those comments Grandma makes about my mom, and I know she doesn't like my mom. But we are family, after all, and we should love each other no matter what. Jesus loves everyone and He tells us to do the same.

Spring has come again. One of the best times for me is when I go alone to our far pasture with our cow. She needs to eat to give us milk every day, and today it is my turn to walk her.

I am wearing a long grey dress with pink flowers and a purple petticoat, and an apron I don't like much, but I wear it because it is easier to wash than my dress. My hair is pulled back into two pigtails and the pink ribbons bob around as I go over to the barn to get Babunia.

We are crossing the long bridge over the Nano River as the late afternoon breeze sways the trees and the sun makes long shadows behind us. A noise coming from under the bridge spooks Babunia and she does not want to cross it. She backs up, stepping heavily on my right foot.

I sit on the side of the road and have a long cry until I don't feel the pain anymore. Then I have a nice talk with our cow. She puts her head down and continues on across the bridge to the other side. She still needs her food so she can give us milk tomorrow morning. The cow seems to feel sorry for me as she picks up her head and starts walking faster. She recognizes the area and starts munching the green grass.

I am glad we have made it here, for now I can relax. I tie the long rope from Babunia's halter to my wrist, and she wanders around and enjoys her dinner while I sit under a huge willow tree with my trusted notebook and write about the bumble-bees buzzing around me. Pretty, colorful butterflies flutter around and land on my shoulder. The bees and butterflies distract me as I rub my sore foot, and I think about being a writer or singer someday. I treasure this time, just me and quiet Babunia. At home I have many jobs waiting for me each day, so this place allows me to dream a little.

I close my eyes and imagine I have lots of friends. I daydream I am a famous person and people like being with me, laughing and having fun. I picture Mom and Dad being my big supporters and they, too, have an easier life somewhere in the big city. It is a nice feeling, even if it is just for this moment.

Babunia is minding her own business, eating the juicy grass around the willow tree. The sounds from the river keep her alert as she picks her head up between bites to listen to the fast and furious running water. Dad tells me every time I come here to stay away from that river. The water here roars and runs deep, showing off who is the boss. Dad reminds me often, "If you ever slip into the river, you would be gone under the current and we wouldn't be able to find your dead body for days and weeks." He was terrified when a twelve-year-old boy from our town drowned in this river last year. Adam was playing with his friends and slipped off the bank, and his body was found more than a week later, two kilometers from the drowning spot.

But my foot is throbbing and I need to cool it down. I remember the last summer when our goat stepped on my foot and Mom soaked it in cold water and it felt better.

Holding a long branch of the willow tree for support, I stick my sore foot in the cold, fast-running river water. It feels good. Then I start to slip lower and lower off the bank toward the rushing river, and I realize I am in trouble. The water is gushing fast, pulling at my petticoats, and if I don't get a miracle soon I will be dragged into the stream. Now I am cold, scared, and feel helpless. There are no homes nearby, and if I yell no one will hear me.

My arms are getting tired from holding the willow branch, and I am praying desperately, asking God to save me. "If You know this is my end, then take me to a better place and save our cow," I pray. "Please send an angel to lift me up if You want me to live. God save me. I'll be a good girl from now on."

My body is getting heavier and heavier as the river pulls at my wet clothing, and now I know I am in really big trouble. My joyous time at the pasture is rapidly turning into a nightmare, and my strength is virtually at the end. I gaze at God's heaven and beg, "Oh God, I am very afraid. Help me to survive this ordeal, pull me up and take me home."

I close my eyes, and suddenly I feel myself floating up to the top of the bank, as if I am in some kind of a dream. What is happening? Is this how it feels to die? No, this cannot be! Here I am, on the top of the river bank. Babunia, who is still tied to my wrist, has dragged me upwards as she moved away from the bank to a better spot to eat.

Getting to my feet, I tell her, "You saved my life. You have saved my life." I kiss her and hug her for what seems to be hours. I tell her how she is such a great cow, and how much I love her.

I look up to heaven and thank my Lord for bringing Babunia to my rescue. I know something wonderful has just happened to me. This has been way too close, and I continue praying and thanking God for saving my life. I promise myself I will not tell anyone, especially my parents, about this accident. If Dad ever found out what happened to me today, he would never let me come here again. I need to be here. This is my quiet and happy place. I think and write and sing songs and dream about a better life somewhere away from here.

Chapter Twenty-Four

I sit at our wooden kitchen table that Dad made for us and stare at the clean utensils in a big blue bowl and the un-matched salt and pepper shakers.

My feet are dangling below the table in my old brown shoes with holes in them. Truth be told, the holes are not that big and water doesn't get in too much, so I am grateful to have them. I had a big smile when Auntie Ginny handed them down from Jana, and they are better than my old shoes.

"One day I will have brand new shoes," I say.

Mom quickly reminds me, "These are good enough to go dancing."

"I will take good care of them," I say.

The school dance is approaching fast and all my friends are looking forward to it. Now I have nicer shoes, but I still have no one to take me. The dance happens only once a year and I hope I will be able to go.

Miss Agnes has asked me to help Tomek, who lives two doors over, with his math homework. He is very nice to me but he is busy helping his dad on the farm and their orchard. Lately he has no time for study, but I am looking forward to spending some time with him soon.

As we walk home from school, I get teased by my two best girlfriends, Josie and Hali, about liking Tomek and doing extra work for him for nothing. I tell them, "When he smiles at me, I feel like my body is made out of jelly and my stomach is doing flip-flops."

"Oh, a sure sign of love," Josie says.

I smile and close my eyes. I try to imagine Tomek and me forever together. I open my eyes and say, "What if I forget how to add?"

Hali says, "One plus one equals two, ha, ha . . ."

"Oh, you guys," I groan. "I'll be fine."

I want Tomek to ask me to go to the dance with him but he keeps avoiding the topic when we are walking home from school. I can't stand it and I wonder if he feels the same way about me.

Last night I was telling Grandma Kula that I don't think I can ever marry anyone who can't make a decision. With her wise years, she comforted me and said, "Sometimes what people do, especially when they are young, it is not the same as who they are later on. Do not fret, my girl, everything will work out as it should. You are not quite eleven years old and have many years ahead of you to think about it."

On the day of the dance I am wearing a blue dress with little white flowers and full sleeves. It has a white detachable collar with rounded corners and buttons in the front to my waist. Grandma puts my hair in pigtails with pink ribbons dangling below my shoulders.

I wait outside for Tomek but he doesn't come out. I walk to school past cousin Joseph's place and I ask Joseph to walk with me to the dance. I am thinking Tomek might not even be at the dance tonight.

Josie and Hali come a bit later with Josie's brother, and all of us hug the lemonade table, looking over our dance prospects.

I finally spot Tomek in the opposite corner standing with his friends. He is very shy and he will not look up. Finally, after a long while, everyone has a dancing partner except me and Tomek. Eventually Tomek gets his nerve and comes over to my side of the dance floor. We look into each other's eyes for what seems like eternity, before we end up on the dance floor.

We barely touch while trying to hold on to each other and move with ease, as the school rules say no dancing too close. The music is slow and the teachers are watching all of us closely.

I don't remember the rest, only that it feels great just to be with Tomek. I am lost in the now, and I don't know how many dances we've had, or what is happening around us. I don't want this moment to end.

Then I see a couple of boys telling others something and the whole classroom roars in laughter. I know it has to be about me, as everyone is staring at me. Lydia from my class taps my shoulder and points.

Mom's face is glued to the window outside, watching.

My heart just about stops, my face is red, and I feel I could crawl under the wood floor we are dancing on. I feel I can almost die from the embarrassment. When I finally get my bearings, I run out as fast as I can.

How could Mom do this to me? I have waited so long to go to this dance, and I might have had a chance to hold hands with Tomek all the way home. Now I am walking home with her. I am so disappointed I won't even talk to Mom. How could she?

Mom insists she is here for my safety. "I know how boys are," she says. "They never are what they seem to be. Don't trust them, they promise you the moon for just a kiss. That is how it all starts, with just a kiss." She goes on and on, like she is an expert on courting or relationships. "You kiss the boy and you get pregnant, that is how it works."

I have never seen my parents embrace or kiss each other. Dad says, "It is dirty to talk about things like that at home." The fear of holding or kissing someone, and that others might judge you for doing something wrong, is unbearable. I don't want to imagine it, for even that is sinful.

Mom tells me she never kissed any boy, not even Dad, until after her wedding, and then she instantly got pregnant with me. I listen to her and nod, and I am getting more scared by the minute about the whole relationship thing.

But even though Mom says I will get pregnant if I hug or kiss a boy, I still want to try that kiss the next time I am with Tomek in our favorite spot.

Dad built the barn out of small cement blocks on the outer edges. It is a tall building with two large doors that open from the middle in the front and two large doors at the back, to drive through with hay and straw. A small side door gets us in and out to retrieve little items. Most days the old rake and shovel lean against the side of the barn and a small wooden ladder stands in the far corner.

The wood is old and dark, with a few layers of paint. A matching fence about five feet tall is attached to the barn and encompasses our whole yard, to keep all the animals in. Dad always seems to be fixing it and replacing the old boards. Stacks of wood are propped up against the other side of the barn, waiting to be used as replacements.

The hay has a musty smell this evening, but it is much softer than the straw. Tomek and I are cuddled in the dim light against the bale of hay. "Close your eyes," I say, "and see what it will be like for us in the future."

"You mean, when we grow up and are going to different schools in the big city?" Tomek asks. We remind ourselves it is only a dream, as we have no means to make it happen.

I want to feel Tomek's skin next to mine. I have begun to unbutton my blouse when we hear voices outside and I panic.

"Krysia!" I hear Mom shout, and I see her shadow coming toward me.

I motion to Tomek and whisper, "Hide, hide behind the bales." Quickly, I button up my blouse with shaky hands and before I am finished, she is shining a small lantern into my eyes and blinding me. "What are you doing here," she demands, "and who are you with? I can see you were up to no good. Who is over there?"

"No one," I say, brushing hay off my clothes.

"Don't lie to me," she continues to shout. "I know he is hiding somewhere here." She lifts the lantern up for a better look. Thank goodness for the shadows everywhere. Tomek is invisible.

Mom pushes me out and locks both doors behind us with a padlock. "If he is hiding inside, he can sleep in the haystack and your Dad will deal with him in the morning."

Inside the house, Mom continues with her accusations. "Do you know where I found her?"

Dad had fallen asleep after he came home exhausted from the farm work, and he is not very happy about being woken up to this sort of complaint. I feel really bad that Mom has to wake him up. I have disappointed him.

He says, "I expect that kind of behavior out of boys but not you. Now everyone in town will be talking about your bad judgement." His look hurts me inside, more than anything else ever before.

"Nothing happened," I say. "I didn't do anything wrong or bad. Why does no one believe me?"

Dad shakes his head and says, "It's getting late. We will talk about this in the morning."

I hope Tomek is alright in the hay barn. I don't want Dad to find him in the morning. Who knows what he will do to him? Also, my tutoring job will be over quickly, as Dad will forbid me to ever see him again.

I lie in bed, thinking. What can I do?

Early in the morning, I quietly take the barn key off the nail rack and try to slip out to use the outside toilet. Mom grabs me by my shoulder as I am opening the door.

"Where do you think you are going at this hour?"

"To the bathroom," I whisper. I don't want to wake up my dad. He has to go to work soon and will be getting up in an hour or so.

"We have a pail in the corner for that," she says as she grabs me tighter.

I say that have to go number two. "My stomach hurts and I need to go now," I add, wriggling out of her clutch and running to the outhouse.

The half-moon-shaped hole above my head is enough to peek through as I stand up on the seat to see if Mom is watching me. She is glued to the window.

I sit on the toilet for a long time, praying that Mom will fall asleep so I can run to the barn and let Tomek out.

After a while, I can't see any sign of her. The birds are singing and the chickens are making noises and it won't be long until Dad will be up and then I will be in more trouble. I run to unlock the barn, and I call softly, "Tomek, wake up, please wake up and go home quickly.'" The barn is dark and scary and no one is moving. I am about to give up and leave when Tomek emerges, very sleepy, and takes off like a shot to the back of the orchard.

"See you later," he shouts.

I am locking the barn door when the light comes on in the house. I run to the outhouse and drop my britches.

I hear shouting from inside the house and Mom is running toward the outhouse. I am greatly relieved when she finds me sitting on the toilet.

That incident was not mentioned again, but it wasn't the end of the trouble I got into with Tomek.

ॐ ॐ

Our finals are approaching, and Tomek and I decide to go to the barn to study for science. Earlier today, our teacher was talking about our bodies and how we can feel different touches and how all the parts of the body work differently. We want to experiment for ourselves how that feels. My parents are not home, so we know we won't be interrupted. We remove our school uniforms and lay them carefully on the hay to keep them clean.

Wearing only my white panties, I stare at Tomek's boxer underpants. We are very serious at first, taking stock of each other's body for our science project. Then we giggle and make silly noises and comments about where the hairs will grow later.

After a long silence we decide to be a doctor and a nurse and take each other's temperature while exploring different parts of our bodies. Things get more interesting when we discover we are made differently. Looking into each other's eyes we embrace and start kissing. Feeling each other's warm body, we have started rolling around when the sound of the barn door opening interrupts us. All at once our neighbor is inside the barn looking at our naked bodies. With his booming voice he shouts, "What are you two doing in here? Get the heck out of here before I tell your parents."

Tomek and I feel judged immediately and we are scared. We know we are in trouble. We gather our clothes and put them on quickly, then run out of the barn like bullets from a gun.

That was when all the bad stuff, the gossip, started happening. This neighbor likes to talk about everything that goes on in our community and this is a juicy story for him. He is the kind of man who will tell every soul in town about this incident. What will happen when Dad hears?

We are doomed, and we know it.

The next day in school is not very pleasant as I am reliving yesterday's nightmare. Kids are pointing fingers at me and making rude comments and laughing behind my back. I am dying inside and want to run far away from here, but I don't have enough money for my fare anywhere. It is a good thing school is almost over for the year.

On the way home, I make a short detour to the railroad station to find out the price to Sosnoviec, the big city where my Auntie Veronica lives with my cousin Ala and her brother Michael. The fare is much more than I have saved, and I know that at this rate I will never save enough money before school is over for the summer.

Everywhere I go, people are whispering. I know they are whispering about me. I want to die, and I hate this small gossipy town. I can hardly wait to run away far from here.

Things will never be the same. Now I look at all the boys very differently and try to imagine if their chest has any hairs or if they have developed any muscles yet. The feeling of wanting to be with Tomek never leaves me. Something about rolling in the fresh hay with my favorite friend in our underwear was wonderful and even if it is wrong it is something I want to do again. But with all the gossip, I'm watched constantly, and scorned.

The train rumbles along, taking me away from the gossips in Topola and away from Tomek. Away from my grandparents, my parents, and my brothers. They will be home for their supper soon, and they will see that I am gone.

I decide I don't want to think any more about my family right now, as it makes me sad that I left and didn't tell anyone where I am going. I close my eyes and imagine my time in Sosnoviec and the hugs that are waiting for me from my cousins, aunt and uncle. *Click clack, click clack,* the train's wheels make noise on the tracks and tick away the time. Only a few more hours and I'll be at their door.

PART III

꙰ 1960 ꙰

Chapter Twenty-Five

❧ ❦

The train has been stopping at towns along the way. Some travelers get off, and others get on. Now, a tall man sits to my right, reading a thick newspaper. His face is mostly covered, as if he is playing hide-and-go-seek. He has an old yellow suitcase, like mine. He reads the paper for a long while without turning a page, and I wonder what is so important that he is looking at it for this long. Is he hiding from me so I don't recognize him?

The trees outside are passing by quickly and I feel queasy. I close my eyes and breathe slowly to settle my tummy. My head is spinning and I think of my parents. God is punishing me for lying to them and running off like that with their money.

Dad will be very disappointed with me for not being honest, and it will put an extra strain on him and Mom with me being away. Who will help look after my two brothers, milk the cow, feed the pigs and chickens, or take our cow to the pasture? What about preparing food for supper, making sauerkraut, pulling the early onions and carrots, picking cucumbers and other vegetables, canning fruit and cleaning the house?

As these thoughts run rampant through my mind, I start to shake and the sweat pours off my forehead. I must have dozed off for a moment, for I am being shaken awake. For a quick moment I'm not sure where I am. The person shaking me is the tall man with the newspaper. Was I talking out loud? Does he know what I did?

He releases me. "Where are your parents?"

Oh, no, here it comes. Lord, don't let me spill all my secrets.

The man is at least my dad's age, maybe older, with a balding spot on the top of his head. He has short, curly hair with a receding hairline and a wrinkled forehead. He is unshaven, and he has big ears. His glasses are quite large, with yellow rims.

His navy jacket with small red stripes, and his red and purple striped shirt with its skinny collar, make me think he works in an office. I notice that his shirt is not tucked into his pants, and I wonder why.

As he sits back, I notice his dark blue pants have stains on the knees, and his short brown boots with dark laces have mud on them. Where was he before he came on the train? We have not had any rain for days.

He is waiting for me to say something. "My parents could not come today," I mumble. "But they will be coming to join me very soon." I can tell from his expression that he thinks I am lying, so I say more. "I am eleven years old and I am old enough to travel by myself. I am going to see my cousin Ala who is ten years old, and her brother Michael who is thirteen, as well as my aunt and uncle. They are very nice and invited me to their place for the summer."

"Aha," he says. "Your parents let you go all alone on this big train all the way to the big city in the middle of the night with ten stops along the way?"

"Yes, they did," I insist. "And I am not scared."

"Do you know what time we will be there?"

"No, and I don't care, as my Auntie Veronica left me instructions how to get there. I know how to read and I will find her house with no problem. See, I have her address right here on this piece of paper."

The man crosses his arms on his chest. "It will be after midnight, and you have to walk a long ways to your aunt's place, dragging your suitcase. I assume it is your suitcase, the way you are holding it so tightly?"

"Yes, it is," I confirm.

"What is in your suitcase?" he asks.

"My clothes, my doll, my songs, and my writing notebooks."

"You can sing and write also?"

"I don't sing, only to our animals, but I do make notes daily."

"What do you write about?"

He is very nosy, but I don't see any harm in telling him about my writing. He seems interested in me and what I do; that's more than most people I know back home.

"Mostly I write about how I feel," I answer, "what makes me sad, and what makes me happy. Also, I try to note the things that happen in our daily lives."

"Wow. You know how to do that?"

"I pray and try to be honest about how things are each day and it helps me to feel better. When I write, I feel like I am talking to my friend. I can say anything I want, and no one tells me otherwise or judges me."

"It must feel good to have a friend to talk to," he says with a strange smile. "I want to be your friend. You can tell me anything you want."

I think about this. Outside the window, the sun is orange and pink and very bright, and I close my eyes. Tomorrow will be a brand-new day at my auntie's place. I love this feeling. With my eyes closed, I pretend I am safe.

"I am Joe," he says. Startled, I open my eyes and see he has his hand stretched out. "And your name is?"

I hesitate, but then shake his hand. "My name is Krystyna. But most people call me Krysia."

"So, what do your parents do? Are they farmers?"

Dad has cautioned me often, and especially when we are among people we didn't know, "Watch out when strangers start asking you about your life. Some think we are dumb farmers who don't know anything because we live on a farm in a small farming town."

"My parents are *educated* farmers," I tell him. "My dad came from Sosnoviec, where he lived with his parents and went to private school. He was very well educated before his parents moved to Topola. They work very hard to provide for us a decent and honest living."

"So you love your parents, but you don't want to stay on the farm to help them for the summer, is that right?"

My look confirms his suspicions. Now my mind is racing as to what to say next. By now, he must have figured out that I am a runaway. What if he gets in touch with my dad and tells him where I have gone, and Dad comes to take me home? My trip will be ruined, and I will have to go home and face everyone.

The train is making another stop. The conductor comes over and asks me, "Is everything alright?"

"I am fine," I say.

Joe tells him, "We are good, she is with me and I am looking after her."

I don't know if that is good or bad, but I nod my head and confirm, "We are fine." More people get off the train, leaving only me, Joe, and one other man at the far end of our car.

The sound of the whistle, huge clouds of gushing steam, and a deep rumbling of the engine, tell me we are about to start moving again. The train moves slowly, passing lots of green fields and little towns along the side of the track, and some people are waving from the fields as if they know me. It is exciting to see that the train whistle toots a special "Hello" to them. In the sky above the trees, the day is declining and the sunset is ready to come on.

"It is getting dark out there," Joe pipes up, "and soon it will be nighttime. Are you scared of the dark?"

"No," I say, but inside I am scared a little, because I don't know this area. "I will be fine."

"Let me walk up with you to make sure you get where you are going."

"No, thank you," I tell him. "I have to do this all by myself."

He smiles, crosses his arms again, and stares at me for a long while.

I open my suitcase for a moment to put away my book full of songs, and then put my suitcase on the floor, next to his. I read my songs earlier and now I hum them under my breath. The train is rocking us back and forth and I am getting sleepy.

"This is my stop," Joe says, picking up his suitcase. "You should come with me."

"I don't want to go with you," I tell him. But he grabs my suitcase and starts for the door. I go after him, crying, "I want my suitcase back."

Then the stranger at the end of the car stands up and says to Joe, "Give back her suitcase." Joe drops my suitcase and hisses, "This is not the last time you will see me." Then he leaves the train.

The stranger is a good-looking man with a dark mustache and large arms. He smiles at me. "You can go back to your seat," he says. "He won't be bothering you anymore."

"Thank you for your help," I say, and he nods before going back to his seat.

I keep my suitcase on my lap for the rest of the way. After midnight, the train finally arrives in Sosnoviec. The conductor comes over and announces, "This is your stop. Let me help you with your suitcase."

I say, "No, thank you, I will handle it myself," as I drag it down the three steps onto the pavement. My ears are plugged from all the noise and I can't see very well.

Looking around the station in the dark of the night with no one to greet me, I start to panic a little. What am I doing here? I should have stayed home helping my parents. What are they going to think of me now?

I see the conductor walking nearby, and I ask him, "Do you know which road I should take to get to Wolver Street?"

He points to the street on the right, which goes straight up the hill. "It is a long hill you have to climb, child, before you get there."

The whistle blows, and I thank him again and assure him, "I will do just fine."

As I watch the train disappear, a cold chill is going right through me. What was I thinking, going on this long trip all by myself in the middle of the night? I start to pray. "God, come with me and guide me safely to my auntie's place."

I am dragging my suitcase along the cobblestone sidewalk. There are no lights on this street. The moon is bright, and it makes dark shadows on the sides of the street. "Please, God," I continue to pray, "stay with me all the way up that big hill and keep me safe until I find my Auntie Veronica's place."

It is hard to say who can see me, out in the moonlight in the middle of the street. Shadows are following me and odd noises add to the mystery that is all around. I walk past a spooky-looking house. The front porch is sagging, the windows have no panes. In the darkness far ahead, I see a dim light flickering.

I keep my head lowered, as my shoes make clicking noises on the cobblestone pavement. A dog barks close by, and when I turn to look in that direction, I stumble and fall. I glance around but see only shadows. Sitting on my suitcase, I rest a bit. I am alright with only a scraped knee, nothing to worry about. Lord, I am already tired, but I have to keep going.

I notice a long shadow on the corner of the next building. It looks like someone is standing there, watching me. I am almost convinced that someone is following me but every time I turn around to see who it is, there is no one.

My heart is beating very fast, my forehead is sweaty, and I am trembling with fear. I close my eyes and pray for safety, and when I open them the shadow is gone. The flickering light ahead has disappeared. It is dark and eerie, but I continue up the hill.

Lord, help me to stay safe.

I keep walking up the big hill, dragging the suitcase with all my possessions. I have to be brave.

My racing mind is flashing back to what my dad said to me many times before: Be careful. Don't tell everyone the details of your life. Don't talk to strangers, as they might use the personal information and come to hurt you or steal you away. What goes on behind our closed doors, stays behind our closed doors.

Perhaps Joe never got off the train; instead, he was hiding in the next car and got off at my station. He did ask a lot of personal questions about where I was going and who was coming to pick me up. Maybe he wants to see where I will be staying and come to do something not nice.

Finally, I cannot stand it any longer and I scream as loud as I can, "You can come out now, whoever you are, and take whatever you want. I don't have much to give you. Quit following me and scaring me!"

I wait, but no one is emerging from the shadows and the night is very dark.

I close my eyes, take a deep breath, and ask God again, "Please continue to walk with me on this journey of mine." All at once, calm comes over me and I am not scared any longer. Deep down in my heart I know I am going to be alright, and my suitcase becomes much lighter. I start to hum songs from Sunday School, and finally I arrive at #451 Wolver Street. I let out my breath and I hope that this is my Auntie Veronica's place at last.

As I turn around and give one last look before knocking on the door, I see the same shadow that followed me from the train station. I am sure of it. Sometimes that shadow was taller and other times I could hardly see it, but it was there.

Perhaps it was my guardian angel.

But maybe not.

Who was that shadow, and what was it after?

Chapter Twenty-Six

❧ ❦

I am here, I am here, I am finally here. I swing the gate open and walk up to the front door of Auntie Veronica's house, thanking God for bringing me here safely.

I knock softly so as not to wake everyone. The house is dark, and I am panicking, wondering if I got the right house after all. I have only seen the address and the small map that Auntie scribbled for me when she visited us many months ago. I am not sure what kind of welcome I will receive at this hour. Auntie Veronica may not recognize me; after all, kids do change a lot, especially when they are very young. But it is too late to turn back.

I hear footsteps and a thump from inside the house. Auntie looks out the window to see who could be at her door at one in the morning. She keeps looking and looking at me, and finally throws her hands up in the air and opens the front door. "What have we here now?"

We stare at each other. "Auntie, Auntie, it is me, Krysia, remember me? You invited me to come and visit you when you were in Topola."

"Oh, my God, bless the Father in Heaven. Where is your daddy?" I know why she is assuming that I came with my dad. My mom would never venture anywhere. She has never been anywhere farther than twenty kilometers from home, except for the hospital in the big city. "Where is your dad?" she asks again.

"I am all alone, Auntie. I came on the midnight train to see you, all by myself."

She stands in the open doorway, holding the doorknob and looking astonished. After a final glance toward her gate, she steps back. "Come in, come in," she whispers. "Let's get you inside." She quickly shuts the door behind me and locks it.

I have never seen my auntie speechless before. She loves life and is well known for telling stories. Maybe when she was visiting, she was just telling me one of her stories, and she didn't really expect me to come to visit her.

"I am glad I remembered your instructions on how to get to your place," I continue.

"You mean the little map I drew on the scrap of paper?" she asks in amazement.

"Yes. I followed your map to the letter and I am here safe. Are you happy to see me?"

"Yes, yes, I am happy that you are here in one piece." Her smile looks worried. "Tomorrow morning we will telegraph your dad to tell him you are here safe." She looks closely at me. "You did tell them you were coming to see me?"

My face must be turning all red. I don't know what to say.

Auntie shakes her head. "Come and have a glass of milk."

She is wearing a blue housecoat with a white collar, and fuzzy pink slippers, and her dark hair is long and braided to one side. "Everyone is asleep," she says. "And we should be going to bed as well. We will talk about all this in the morning."

I give her a big, long hug, and after a while she finally loosens my hands off her waist.

"I am so glad I found your place," I say again. "You did give me good directions, and I remembered them."

Auntie shakes her head again. "Come to bed, my child. That pail in the corner is for your bathroom break, if you need to go in the night. Tomorrow, I will show you our outhouse behind the shed."

Auntie's house has two rooms. In this one there is a long kitchen table with four actual matching chairs against the wall to the right, and a large stove to the left. The cabinet is white with many shelves that hold lots of dishes on them. There are delicate lace curtains in the windows. In the bedroom, I see the same lace curtains, two small beds pushed together, and two dressers with drawers on the far-right wall. In the left corner is a small, black potbelly stove to heat the house.

The beds are pushed together. Michael and Ala are asleep on one of them. Auntie hands me one of Ala's nightshirts. "Your Uncle Henry is away for work most of the summer, so there is room for you with us."

I put on Ala's nightshirt, wash my face and hands in the basin on the table, and crawl into bed. I can feel Ala's breathing beside me. Auntie Veronica climbs in and puts her arm around me and we say our prayers quietly together, thanking God for the miracle of my safe journey to her place. "We will talk tomorrow," she says, as she strokes my pigtails. "We'll talk tomorrow."

I snuggle up to Ala, but my eyes are wide open. I am thinking about that shadow that was following me all the way here.

Sleeping with the three of them squashed together reminds me of when I used to share my bed with my brothers, before I asked for my own space behind the dresser. I feel love and contentment. I don't want this night to end. Tomorrow I have to face the horror of revealing all my secrets, which will send me back home on the next train. My mind is racing.

What would be the best way to handle this situation?

Was the shadow Joe, the man from the train?

What if he is a killer—or worse? He knows now where I am staying and he might return tomorrow.

Are my parents worried about me? Do they know about the neighbor finding me with Tomek in the barn?

What will Auntie say when I tell her?

I don't know which thoughts are worse, the ones about the shadow or the ones about why I have run away from home and how I will have to explain to my auntie why I am here. The last thing I remember before I fall asleep is asking God, "Please help me with my story tomorrow."

∼ ∽

Banging in the kitchen wakes me up in the morning. When I open my eyes, I see both Ala and Michael standing by the bed and staring at me. "Hello cousins," I mumble and they smile politely.

"Hello to you, too," says Ala. "Breakfast is ready if you are up for it." She is one year younger than me but much smaller.

As I slip out of bed I want to fall on my knees and thank God in heaven for bringing me to this place. I straighten Ala's nightgown and hurry to the kitchen table. A big smile from Auntie Veronica is welcoming and comforting. She points to a chair and says, "Sit down and have some beans and bread with honey." She pours me some milk.

I am very hungry, though I didn't even know it until I put the bread in my mouth. The last time I ate was yesterday morning at our farm.

"Can I show Krysia our rabbits, can I, can I?" asks Ala.

"Sure you can, after you do your chores," says Auntie. "Krysia and I need to have a little talk first."

I am not looking forward to our talk. As soon as Michael and Ala go outside, I start to talk about anything and everything except why I am here. "Beautiful day," I pipe up. "How many chickens do you have? What kind of fruit do you grow? How is your garden doing? Do you still have your beehives and how many? Where is Ala's and Michael's school? How far is the church you attend?"

I am just about out of breath, and she is not answering any of my questions.

Here we go, I think. This is where I spill my guts about my wagon trip, getting caught with the neighbor boy in the haystack, and that everyone in town hates me and laughs at me and that I don't want to live there anymore. Also, that I took Dad's money and that I don't want to go back home ever again.

Auntie is making tea. "Tell me everything that happened in Topola that would make you come all the way to our place."

I stand up. "Let me do the pouring, Auntie. I do it at home all the time." As I pour the tea, the top of the teapot rattles.

"Don't be nervous," she reassures me. "Just come and sit so we can have that chat. Now, let's have it."

Oh, God, where do I begin? Which part do I leave out? Oh, well, here it goes. I am shaking inside. The clock is ticking loudly in the next room and I am very distracted. I want to run from here or I want to disappear. I wish Ala would walk in and ask me to go outside to play with her. She is busy feeding her rabbits. Michael has gone to see his friends, and Auntie and I are all alone. I am relieved when she gets up to tend to the stove, as something is cooking for lunch.

The kitchen is about half the size of the bedroom, but much warmer. There is always something cooking on the stove. Old linoleum with brown squares covers the floors, but it is nice and shiny. We have a dirt floor in our house, so this is like being in first class already. Back home, folks talk about people in the big cities living the high life with no dirt floors.

"Snap out of it, Miss Krysia," Auntie says. "Are you day-dreaming or what?" I am scared to open my mouth, so I clench my tummy and pretend that it is upset and hurting. I muster, "I think I am going to be sick."

"Now, now," she says. "We can do this later. It must be the late night you had."

"That must be it," I agree, and she helps me back to the bedroom.

"Lay down for a while until your body calms down. We will talk after lunch."

In bed I am worried sick. What will happen after our talk? Will she send me back home tomorrow, or send a telegram to my dad to come and get me? I close my eyes and I feel like I am falling down a long spiral tunnel. "God help me to stay here," I pray. Thoughts are running through my head and I can't quiet them down. What am I doing? I have to tell the truth sooner or later. Why am I putting this off?

What about my parents, grandparents and my brothers? Are they looking for me? They wouldn't think that I could come all this way by myself, would they? They must be worried sick by now. Are they running around to the homes of our cousins, aunts, and uncles to see if I am there? Maybe they think the gypsies stole me from our house.

I must get Auntie Veronica to send a telegram to our town's postal office, so they can deliver it to my parents. But wait, wait a minute. If I tell them where I am, Dad will be here in a few hours and my time in a big city will be over. I am not ready to face all the demons back home. Oh, what have I done? What should I do now?

I finally fall asleep.

I wake drenched with sweat and screaming with fear. I sit up, trying to blink away the terrifying vision. Auntie opens the bedroom door. She says, "Don't worry, my child, it was only a dream. Everything will be alright. Go wash up and get dressed. Then, please go outside and tell Michael and Ala to come in and wash up for lunch."

"Yes, Auntie," I answer, still shaking. I open my suitcase to get out clean clothes and gasp in horror. The suitcase is full of papers and official books. That nosy man on the train, Joe, must have switched our suitcases. I wonder if he did that on purpose!

Thoughts swirl in my head. Why did he switch our suitcases? Who is he and where is he from? Is he going to surprise us in the middle of the night? What will he do to me when he finds me?

Oh no! My writings, all my worldly possessions were in my suitcase. Will I ever see them again? What about my clothes and my favorite nightshirt? What am I going to do now?

What will I change into?

I push the suitcase back under the bed and decide I will have to wear the clothes I wore yesterday.

A beautiful, sunny sky greets me outside, and Ala shows me the rabbits and chickens. We also check for any eggs.

"Do you have special names for your chickens and rabbits?" I ask.

Ala shakes her head. "No, we don't. We only have two chickens and two rabbits, and one of them has floppy ears. Let's go and feed them so I can introduce you to them."

The yard is clean and tidy, with flowers all around the sidewalk and under the windows. A brick sidewalk leads to the front steps. The back yard has two pens, one for chickens and one for rabbits. Two fruit trees make a nice shade in the afternoon sun. The cherry tree is almost ready for picking and the apple tree is in bloom.

I ask, "Where do the bees live that make your delicious honey?"

"Down by the gravel pit, on a friend's property," Michael tells me. "He lets us keep our beehives there and we give him some honey in return. I can take you there after lunch," he adds.

"Are the chickens and rabbits the only chores you have?" I ask.

Ala and Michael look at me, and Ala asks, "Why, do you have more chores on your farm?"

"Yes, I do, at home and on the farm. From early in the morning to late at night until we drop into our beds from exhaustion."

"When do you get to play?" Michael asks.

"We play with our animals when we feed them and clean them, or when we take our cow to the pasture land about two kilometers from home."

"Sounds like living on the farm is exhausting," Ala says.

"Let's go check out our bees and I will show you how they live," Michael says.

"What about lunch? I was supposed to call you inside to wash up before we eat. Your mom must be ready for us by now."

Michael grabs my hand and says, "We will be back in a few minutes. Mom won't even miss us. Let's go now."

We run to the gravel pit, skipping on the dirt road. "I am very happy that I finally get to meet you two in person and play with you," I say. "On your mom's last visit to Topola, she told me lots about you guys and I feel like I already know you well."

Here I am holding hands with my two distant cousins and enjoying God's beautiful sunshine with not a care in the world, for at least a few minutes. I almost forget all about where I have come from and what happened there. I don't have to do a million chores here, like every day at home. No one is pointing fingers at me or laughing at me and judging me.

As we walk home, I hope Auntie has forgotten about our talk and we can put it off until tomorrow. But as we approach the house, Auntie runs out and calls to us, "Quick, come in, I have something to tell you."

We sit down quietly and I am terrified of what will unfold next. I am sure it is all about me and why I am here. "Where were you so long?" Auntie asks. "The neighbor down the road, Emilia, had a bad spell, and her son wants me to go and sit with her. Heat up some soup and stay around the house. I don't know how long I'll be gone."

"Stay as long as you need to," I tell her. "I will make us some supper if I have to. I know how to cook."

Auntie hurries out the door.

Phew. I breathe much easier as it wasn't about me after all. We have soup for lunch and play with the rabbits and chickens. I show them how to play hide-and-go-seek around their trees and shrubs until we are exhausted.

"The neighbor must be bad off for Mom to stay out this late," Michael says.

I cook some potatoes and carrots with fried onions for supper. After we eat, we tell a few stories to each other before we get ready for bed. I have to wear the nightdress Auntie loaned me. I don't know what I am going to do about my suitcase. I won't think about that right now.

At night, when everyone in the house is sound asleep, I go outside, needing the bathroom. I don't worry about finding my way through the house, as Auntie has a small lantern in the kitchen. The light is low all night, making shadows in the rooms. I come outside with bare feet, collecting dew on the soles.

It is always a relief to empty my bladder. "Better than sex," that's what my older cousin says. As good as it feels, though, I sincerely hope she is wrong.

While I am getting back into bed, my auntie comes home. "Thank you for looking after them and for cleaning up the kitchen," she says. "Everything seems to be in order, so let's get some sleep."

After we are done with our prayers, we say the Hail Mary and cross ourselves. Then I close my eyes and talk to God. "Help me to know what to do and say. Forgive me for all my sins. Love people like me and love Auntie and her family. Make us happy and safe and make the world a better place. Amen."

Chapter Twenty-Seven

I wake up quite late to a bright sunny morning and run straight outside. I say, "Thank you again, God, for bringing me here safely." Rain has fallen overnight, but the sun is out, shining on the tiny beads of water that still cling to the fruit trees and the flowers. What a lovely and fresh day unfolding before me.

Auntie loans me Ala's apron to wear while I am helping with house chores and meals. The morning goes by quickly.

After lunch Auntie says, "Let's go sit outside on the bench, smell the fresh air, and have our talk." I nod nervously and give her my half smile.

Auntie's flowers are lovely and smell kind of sweet. Birds are singing their afternoon songs. I watch a beautiful butterfly on a pink flower flapping her wings, and my mind starts to wander. Oh, it is so peaceful here. I could live like this forever. The truth will be difficult to tell her, but it has to be told sooner or later. It would be great with me if it was much, much later, like a few months from now.

Auntie takes my hand and jolts me back to the present. "How are your parents and grandparents?"

"They are just fine and working really hard," I say. "But they have no time to spend with me."

Auntie nods. "It is that time of the year on the farms, where everyone is very busy and forgets to be together and just do nothing." Auntie always has something nice to say about every situation, and it is one of the reasons I like her very much. She also doesn't talk down about my mom, like Grandma does. "So tell me, what made you come and see me?" She sounds honestly interested.

"I wanted to see you and my cousins and life in the big city." I sit up straighter and taller, my heart starting to beat so fast I can hear it in my ears. I clear my throat; this is it and there is no turning back. I can feel Auntie's knee barely touching mine. A full minute passes without either of us saying a word. I am feeling perfectly happy that I am here, and now this confession. I would rather clean our pig stalls than spill my guts to Auntie.

Auntie gives me a reassuring smile. "Just take your time and tell me what happened. Why did you leave your home?"

I take a deep breath. "I got caught with a boy next door in our hay barn practicing our biology class, and the neighbor discovered us and was telling the whole town about us," I say, embarrassed. "Then there was the horrible trip to Topola with Ed the wagon driver, who is now looking for me, to do who knows what to me."

I feel a lump gather in the back of my throat and my eyes fill with tears. Auntie reaches for my hand and says, "Go on, child, it is alright, I am here for you."

I start sobbing uncontrollably and I can't stop. She opens her arms to me and I lean into them and feel them close around me. She holds me tight and assures me again, "Everything will be just fine." It feels so good to be in her arms and I don't ever want her to let go of me. It feels special and comforting beyond any words.

Auntie pats me on the back and says, "Come on now, stop crying, everything is going to work out." Her hands feel warm on my back and I feel her heart throbbing against my chest as she continues to rub my back. I let out my breath, realizing I have been holding it for a while. I lift my head after what seems like forever, and I open my eyes and look at Auntie's gentle face. Her look reassures me.

"And," I continue, "the worst part is how I wish I had a mom to talk to, but she is always thinking about other things like the babies that died, and not getting to be a nun, and not having enough money for anything. I have been secretly helping a neighbor with sewing and saving all my money for the trip to see you. But I didn't have enough money for the ticket so I borrowed some from my dad without telling him. He gave it to me to pay the store owner on our account and I didn't do that. I used it for the ticket to come here."

Now I feel very scared. My secrets are all spilling out, like a garbage truck has backed up and dumped its dirty contents for me to sort out. But that isn't the worst and most frightening thing that has happened to me. And it is even worse because Auntie is looking off toward the trees, looking at nothing and thinking. We sit on the white wooden bench, my feet dangling down, while she stares into the distance, not saying a word. I know she is digesting the things I just told her, and she is nodding, like she is agreeing with her thoughts.

I feel sticky air all around us. My neck is sweating, and my hands are clammy and folded together like in prayer. I might as well be praying fast and hard for forgiveness and asking to be allowed to stay here a little bit longer. I am sniffling and wiping my cheeks. My nose is running, too. And there is still no motion from Auntie. Now that I have finished spewing out every horrible thing about me, if she can only forgive me and accept me, I will be okay. I want to tell her about Joe, too, but I am already afraid I have said too much.

Finally, Auntie stands. She gives me her hand and pulls me up from the bench. "Krysia, you are a hard-working little girl and you are a good person. I learned early in life that you cannot please everybody, but you have to listen to your heart and make smart choices." Her hug is even bigger than before, and I feel dizzy from her love. "We both need a little breather," she continues. "I will go inside to get a glass of lemonade for us."

The lemonade is cool and sweet and we drink it in silence. The sky getting darker, and shadows of the drooping tree limbs moving on the half-lit porch.

After supper, I am tidying up the kitchen when Ala runs to answer the front door. She comes back with a confused look on her face. "There is a man, a very tall man, at the door to see you," she tells me.

"Who is it?"

"He says his name is Joe and he has your suitcase. Is that true?"

I nod and start praying under my breath, "Father, God, help me get through this," as I walk to the front door.

There he is, on the steps right outside the front door, smirking at me. "Hello, Krysia, how have you been? Did you miss me?"

He is talking like we are old friends or something. "Fine," I squeak out and I don't smile back.

"I am sorry for scaring you like that when I was getting off the train. In all the commotion that was happening, I must have grabbed the wrong suitcase. So sorry."

I feel my eyes tearing up and I lower my face, so he can't see I'm upset.

"So, tell me, how you are enjoying your vacation?" he continues.

Auntie Veronica had been lying down to rest, but now she is coming to see who I am talking to. "Hi, my name is Veronica, and you are . . . ?"

"Good evening, Miss Veronica, I am Joe. From the train. I have brought Krysia her suitcase. I must have grabbed it by mistake as we both have the same kind."

Auntie Veronica smiles and says to me, "Maybe we could invite the nice man for a glass of lemonade?"

I quickly say, "He has to go. I mean, he can't stay. He has important things to do."

"Alright then," says Auntie Veronica, "but we do have plenty." She goes to finish tidying up the kitchen.

"I will get your suitcase," I say to Joe. "Just stay here."

When I return with his suitcase, he has gone down the steps and is standing on the sidewalk below. He is scanning the entire yard and smiling to himself. He is still holding my suitcase.

"I hope I find everything in my suitcase as I left it," I say sternly.

"Me too," he says, as he continues to look toward the back yard. "You seem to be very comfortable here. How long are you staying?"

How is it his business how long I am staying? Is he planning to come back again, or surprise us in the middle of the night or something? "My daddy will be here tomorrow to get me," I blurt.

"Well then, this is our official goodbye." He comes back up the steps and leans over to hug me.

I move back, pushing his suitcase toward him and holding my hand out for mine. "Goodbye to you too." I grab my suitcase from him, go inside, and close the door tight behind me. I look through the window to make sure he is leaving. He waves goodbye with a nasty smile that sends chills up my spine.

I have an uneasy feeling that I will see him again, and that is a very disturbing thought. Now I'll have to watch over my shoulder the entire time I am here.

After I make sure everything is still in my suitcase, I go to the kitchen to help Auntie finish cleaning up before we go to bed. She looks through the window to the back yard. "Shift in the weather, I feel coolness in the air." She closes the window and smiles at me. "Every person on the face of the earth makes mistakes, Krysia; we are all human. We make the mistakes, but the best part is we get to fix them as well." She hesitates, then adds, "Someday, you will be very amazing, but today you need a little more growing up."

I look at Auntie with my sad eyes.

"Thank you for telling me why you ran away from your parents. They must be very worried. Tomorrow we will contact them and tell them that you are alright."

I start to cry. "After all the misery I have caused, I'll just sit here and enjoy being alone."

"Don't sit too long. Go to bed soon and get some rest." She bends over, kisses my forehead, and says, "Goodnight, Krysia. There is nothing perfect in this world, there is only life."

Auntie always has great things to say. Thank you, Lord, for this trying day.

Chapter Twenty-Eight

୬ ୬

The next day, Michael is reading us a story about bees as the three of us we walk toward the hives. Honeybees are social insects and live in colonies, he tells us. Each colony is a family unit, made up of a queen bee and her workers. All worker bees gather food, build nests and look after baby bees. The queen bee doesn't do anything, only lays eggs.

It is quiet and peaceful around here. I could live here forever with Michael, Ala, and Auntie Veronica. I could go to school with my cousins and enjoy the city life. My cousin Michael is very smart and good looking. He is also three years older than me. Every time I look at him I forget where I am.

"You haven't heard a word I am reading, have you?" Michael has stopped walking. "What are you thinking?"

"What? Oh, I am not thinking of anything in particular, just enjoying our walk," I say.

In the field are many tall white boxes spread around and standing like soldiers. "Wow, so many of them!" I am surprised.

"We have to check on them every few days," says Michael. "People around here like our bees, because of all the pollinating they do. They make their cucumbers much bigger and help pollinate all the beautiful flowers around here."

"The flowers are beautiful," I agree.

"That buzzing sound coming from the hives is all the bees at work making honey for us. Send them your love and they won't sting you."

I close my eyes and keep sending love to all the bees. I start to think again about me living here forever.

A tap on my shoulder startles me.

"Come," says Michael, stretching out his hand for mine. "Let's go down to the gravel pit."

We go down the embankment, behind the big pile of small gravel rocks. We jump and play hide-and-go-seek, and talk. Ala is bored and she wants to go home.

"I don't want to go, not yet," I tell her. I don't want this day to end.

"Well, I am going home anyways," Ala says. She turns around and walks away, and I stand to follow Michael, who is flicking small rocks at the hill.

Then I freeze.

Joe is on the far end of the gravel pit looking at me from the edge of the bush. It is definitely him. His stare is paralyzing. "My life is over now," I keep repeating to myself. "My life is over . . ."

Michael looks back at me. "What's wrong, Krysia?"

"Only everything," I squeak. I start running as fast as I can through the bushes and the trees and finally trip over a rotten log. After that, I don't remember anything.

When I open my eyes, I am completely pinned down and I can't breathe. Someone is on top of me. He has his hand on my face and I can't see anything.

Joe.

I will never see my parents or grandparents ever again. I am going to die.

I start praying under my breath, "Oh, Lord, if this is your will for me, then take me now. But if this isn't your will for me, please let me live and I'll never do anything like this again. I will be more careful in the future and I won't tell any strangers personal details of my life."

I try to scream for Michael. Where is he?

Joe's cologne is nauseating and I can hardly breathe. He is grabbing my hair and kissing me on the cheeks and my forehead. When he finally moves his hand enough I scream, "Help, help!"

"Be quiet," he tells me. "There is no one around to save you. There are only the two of us here and that's how I want it."

I tell myself Michael has gone for help and will be back soon. Joe must know that and he just wants to scare me. I hope and pray this is true.

My mind races. I had been too scared to tell Auntie Veronica what had happened on the train, as I didn't want to be a burden. Now I wish I had come clean and told her everything about Joe, so I wouldn't be trapped in this situation.

I can hear people talking in the distance. They are coming toward us. Joe muffles my mouth and tells me, "Be quiet if you know what is good for you. After all, I know where you are staying." Then he gets up and disappears into the bushes, and I start to scream and call out. I sit up.

Michael, Auntie Veronica, and her neighbor come over to me at once.

Michael asks, "Are you okay?"

"Thank God nothing serious happened to you," Auntie says, looking at my head. "Can you walk?"

When I nod, my head hurts and I burst into tears. I try to tell Auntie Veronica about Joe, but she says, "Save your strength.

Let's get you home where you can rest for a while, and we'll talk later."

෯ ෯

Auntie Veronica comes into the bedroom to tell me she has lunch waiting. "Come and have some boiled eggs and really good tea with honey the way you like." The honey does make the tea taste much nicer than the sugar from our sugar beets at home. But right now I want to tell her about Joe.

"Auntie," I start.

"Just enjoy your tea," she says. "After lunch, we need to have a talk about what we are going to do with you."

I can hardly swallow my eggs. I keep thinking that this is it, it is over and I am going home. I don't even want to think about what my dad will do to me when he gets here.

I eat very slowly to stretch the time.

After the dishes are done, we go out to Auntie's garden and settle ourselves on the wooden bench. She checks the bump on the back of my head again, and then she takes my hand. "After we talked yesterday, I sent the telegram to your parents so they'll know where you are and that you are safe with us. I did ask your dad if they could let you stay with us for a little longer, to give both of you a short break. We should have his answer by tomorrow or the next day."

I get up and hug my auntie real hard. "I will be really good and I'll help a lot around here," I mumble with my face pressed against her tummy. "Thank you, thank you, my dear auntie, for allowing me to stay a little longer." I hope my parents will agree.

෯ ෯

Morning has come early. The birds are singing, the sun is shining, and it promises to be a great day.

As we are doing our chores outside, a young man on his bicycle approaches the house and says, "I have a telegram for Veronica."

Michael takes it from him and calls his mom. Auntie reads what it says and looks very seriously at me. "You can stay a bit longer with us before your dad comes to get you."

I smile at her and say, "Thank you once again, I do appreciate your generosity."

Later, Michael announces, "I want to show you something. Let's go for a walk to see an old house in the bush, behind our neighbor's property."

On a hill in the forest, I see a small hut below. I follow Michael cautiously, and as we make our way downhill through the thick trees something stings me on my calf. I make a screeching noise. "Be quiet," Michael warns me. "Someone might hear us."

Through the hut's window, we see an oil lamp burning on the small table, but no one seems to be inside. Michael says, "Let's go inside and see who lives here."

Hesitantly, we creep inside the dim room. The place is very messy and has one window, a tiny bed, a table, and a potbelly stove in the middle.

I whisper, "Let's get out of here. This is private property and we'll get in trouble if the owner finds out we are snooping around."

As we walk out the door a large, unkempt looking man jumps out of the bush, shouting at us. "What are you doing here, snooping again?" He scares us half to death, but then he runs away in the opposite direction.

Michael grabs my hand and we run for home as fast as we can. "Look out for the snakes," he warns me. I am afraid of snakes, so now I am stepping high and running blindly. My heart is beating so fast, I feel like it is going to jump out of my chest.

We finally reach the edge of Michael's property. We sit on the old wooden bench to calm down before entering the house.

"That man, he looked and sounded like a madman," I muster.

"City folks say he is not right," Michael says, putting his arm around me. "He ran away when he saw us. He was just as scared of us as we were of him."

"We won't tell your mom we went there," I say. I don't want her to be disappointed in me. She might send me home right away.

"This will be our secret," Michael agrees.

I feel safe with Michael, and before I know it I am telling him about Joe. "I didn't see him there," Michael says. "I should not have left you while you were unconscious."

"Thank you again for coming to my rescue." I shudder. "I sometimes think he is still around, watching me."

Michael's face is very serious. He says telling Auntie would make her worry. "If he ever comes back, my friends and I will make him sorry. I will look out for you from now on."

His comments are soothing and I keep my head on his chest for a while before going inside the house.

Chapter Twenty-Nine

I am looking forward to today's adventure with Michael. After church, he is taking me to see their river. It is a long walk, all the way to the other side of the city. As long as I am with Michael, the long walk will be fine.

The church is full today and the priest leads us in prayer for blessings on our lives, our homes, our land, and our country. Some people are whispering, murmuring to God, as we kneel to say our prayers. It sounds like a swarm of bees buzzing around us.

Mass is about to commence and dozens of candles cast a warm glow throughout the church. After we have started our hymns, someone staggers in, plopping with a thud in the wooden pew directly behind me.

I can smell the alcohol, just as I have smelled it many times before on my dad's breath. I glance over my shoulder to see a man around thirty years old sitting alone in the pew, a drunken smile on his unshaven face. Uncombed hair and a torn t-shirt suggest he doesn't belong here. Judging by many nervous stares in his direction, he is making the congregation uncomfortable. Who is he, and why is he here?

The organist is leading the congregation who have joined the choir of celebration. My cousin Michael goes back to sit with the man, and helps him find the hymns. With each song, the off-key stranger sings with more vigor. He can't sing very well but he looks like he is enjoying himself. My glances make him smile more. As I watch him having so much fun in God's house, my heart begins to soften, and once in a while I trade smiles with him. After all, our God is his God too.

I start to imagine his family, his brothers and sisters, his parents and grandparents. Where are they? Did he run away like I did, and has he no place to stay? Does he live on the streets? How come he is all alone, and seems to be lost? Maybe he came to our church to seek refuge.

Suddenly, in the middle of the sermon something happens. To my right an older man slouches down and slides sideways onto the pew. A couple of people race toward him.

"He is slipping away," says the priest. "Someone please get a doctor."

Some of us are still sitting while others stand around, all feeling helpless. I can't tell if the man is even breathing. Then I hear the stranger ask in a loud voice, "Why don't we all pray for this nice man?"

His words are like a slap on the face. It gets very quiet in the church. Many of us start to pray. I am praying really, really intensely and more sincerely than ever before, with my eyes shut tight.

As I open my eyes, I can't believe what I see. The older man is sitting up. He was lying there not breathing a few minutes ago, but now he is assuring us that he is fine. He says, "I am not going anywhere with the doctor until the service is over."

I hurry to the back of the church and get a glass of water for the man. His sparkling eyes lock onto mine and his smile assures me he is going to be alright, at least for now.

After the commotion, I turn around to see where Michael had been sitting with the stranger, but they are both gone. Who was the man? Where did he go? And where is Michael?

After the benediction, the service is over and I hurry outside. Michael is standing on the church steps. He tells me he felt peace when he was sitting beside the stranger, and wanted to know who he was. But Michael couldn't find him.

No one had seen him leave. It is as if he appeared out of nowhere and then simply vanished. A dying man was revived, saved from death by a prayer initiated by a stranger. What a great God we have.

We all walk home, still talking about the stranger.

After lunch, Michael and I set out on our adventure. To get to the river we have to cross through a long series of pastures with many ditches, where we see geese and a few wild turkeys. Michael takes my hand. "Let's walk faster so we can get there sooner," he says. "I will catch you if you stumble."

Finally we get to the fast-running river, and I gasp. I see something large, struggling in that rapid water. Some kind of animal is fighting for its life.

Michael is quick to run to the nearest stand of trees, where he finds a big branch. He yells, "Come and hold my hand so I don't fall." He extends the branch toward the animal. We can't seem to reach the middle of the river, but we keep trying.

The animal is fighting and scrambling, and finally it gets caught up in a low bush that is hanging into the water. We pull our branch that way so it can climb up.

"It's a dog, it's a dog," says Michael as we pull it up on the bank. The dog is shaking badly. It is frightened and cold. We hold the dog close between us and rub its wet fur.

"Where did you come from?" I ask the dog. "Where is your home?" There are no houses close by, and no one is walking along the river.

"He is a male dog," Michael announces. "He might have slipped into the water a long way up."

"What are we going to do with him?" I wonder.

"I think we have to take him home with us," says Michael. "We can't leave him here like this. Mom will be upset with me, but I have no choice."

We are walking across the pastures and the dog is following us closely. Michael says, "I always wanted to have a dog, but with not much money to feed an extra animal and a small back yard, bunnies were my limit. As Mom says, we could eat the bunnies when they get older, but what does a dog do?"

I see he is happy that he may finally get to have a dog. But now I worry that Auntie may send me home earlier, as she will have another mouth to feed.

Michael's house is not too far now, and I start to pray. "Jesus, please help Auntie want to keep this dog for Michael and please keep me here for a while longer."

The trees are rustling back and forth as we walk and I keep looking back, feeling like someone is following us. I think about Joe and walk faster. The sun is going down quickly and making shadows everywhere. Dusk is approaching as we reach home.

"What have we here now?" Auntie asks. We explain how we got the dog and why we brought him with us. She looks down at the dog, with his head tilted to one side and his droopy eyes, and says to Michael, "Alright, we will keep the dog under one condition. You are totally responsible for taking care of him. You will feed him, walk him, and clean him."

Michael is so happy, he would agree to just about anything. He says, "Yes Mom, I'll look after him."

I can't help but smile to myself, and I think that today Jesus walked with us and protected us. He made things work out for Michael and me, for the dog, and for the stranger from our church. "Thank you, Lord."

Chapter Thirty

~⇠ ⇢~

I am feeling so grateful to Auntie Veronica for letting me stay here for the summer. Over the past couple of weeks I have had the chance to get to know my auntie and cousins well. When I do chores for Michael, he smiles at me and it melts my heart. I play card games with him in the garden. His friends mostly chase each other and tell funny stories, but not Michael. He is more serious than his friends.

Uncle Henry travels out of the city with his sales job, and he is away for a few weeks at a time. Michael sometimes acts as if he is in charge of the whole family. Then his mom lets him know where he stands in the pecking order.

One day, Michael and I are in the back garden. I am telling him how much fun I have been having with him. He wraps his arms around me, and I hug him back.

Then Michael steps back and says, "I like you better than any other girl I have ever known, but you are my cousin, and I know better than to encourage this kind of friendship with you." He looks sad, and all I want to do is kiss him and feel safe in his arms forever. But he is right, we have to be strong and not do any more things like this in the future.

I tense up, as if all of a sudden someone is watching us. Sweat is trickling down my face. Fear comes over me and I feel embarrassed.

Michael says, "Let's go see the bees." He stretches out his hand to me. The sun beats down, lighting up the tips of the picket fences as we walk toward the bees. We share a hopeful glance. Michael squeezes my hand and says, "I still want to look out for you. Are you alright?" I blush but love the attention from him as it makes me feel wanted.

"I am very grateful for our friendship," I tell him. After inspecting the beehives, we walk home quietly and finish our chores.

In the evening, a breeze moves through the room from the open window. I stare out at the dark fringe of the trees by the edge of the woods, thinking about Michael. It is the weird nature of the world to go on spinning, no matter what is happening with us. A half-moon is wedged in the sky like a gold coin into a slot, as the dusk falls.

The next afternoon I watch Ala as she pours more oil on her legs and rubs it all in. She is already so greasy I can almost see my reflection. Her face is red and swollen in the afternoon's hot sun. She blows upwards to get her long bangs out of her eyes, but the hairs are stuck to her forehead. "Hello Cousin, come and join me," she says, like nothing has happened between us.

Ala has ratted me out to her mom. "Michael and Krysia were holding hands and hugging each other. I couldn't hear what they were saying, but it was some kind of secret. Also, yesterday they told me to go away or walk by myself behind them, as they were whispering to each other at the gravel pit."

Auntie looked at Michael. "What were you thinking?"

For the first time, Auntie Veronica was upset with me. I don't want to upset my auntie. She has been a godsend to me these past few weeks. I couldn't look at Michael. All I could do was put my head down in shame. "I promise I will never do that again and I will stay away from Michael from now on." I know this will be hard, because I love being with Michael.

I am very grateful when she says, "Go outside to play, and remember how to behave." It is much too hot outside for me, and I tell myself I have more important things to worry about than Ala. But I go outside anyway.

Now I keep walking past Ala and her oily mess. I skip down the cobblestone sidewalk to the back of the house. Michael is sitting at the outside table with two friends, playing cards. I toss my pigtails back over my shoulders and send them a nice smile.

Michael gathers up the cards, saying, "Let's go to the gravel pit, guys," leaving me and Ala behind.

Ala comes over and says, "I am sorry I told my mom on you and Michael. Please be my friend. You always go somewhere with Michael and don't play with me."

I think about all the times Michael and I wouldn't play with Ala, and how that must have made her feel. She smiles at me, and we start to chase pretty butterflies.

A few days later, I am lying on my stomach, enjoying the sunshine in the back yard, when something moves near my shoulder. I turn my head to see Ala reaching for my notepad. "What is it that you are always writing about?" she asks.

I take it from her. "I will show you later."

"Fine," she says. She slams the door on her way inside.

That was way too close. I'll have to guard the notebook with my life from now on.

Last week, I wrote about when Ala was wearing her white dress with the ruffles around her neck and wrists. Auntie Veronica told her, "Girls dress like that only to go to church, and since there is no service tonight, I can't imagine where you could be going. Take off that dress and go feed your rabbits." Ala will be angry with me for writing about that, and she will tell Auntie everything else I have written about, too. That pad has everything in it, my whole life story. Ala would spill the beans to the whole world.

Next morning, I have just gotten dressed when I realize my notepad is missing. A slow tinge of panic is working its way up my spine. I remember putting it in the pocket of the apron I share with Ala. Then, out of the kitchen window, I see Ala running away from the house wearing the apron. She is carrying something in her hand. I race through the door and down the sidewalk to catch her. My stomach is doing flip flops, and I feel like throwing up. "Oh God, please let me catch her before she has the opportunity to read about the reason I am here."

Ala is almost at the gravel pit when I get near enough to call to her. "Ala, wait for me."

She does have my notebook. I can see it in the pocket of the apron.

"Oh, thank goodness you have my notebook," I tell her. "I have been looking all over for it."

"I didn't notice it when I put the apron on this morning," she lies, handing it to me. "What's so important about it that you had to run all the way here?"

"It is only some notes I make occasionally for my school project. Things I have done on my school vacation this summer."

"Can you show me?"

"It isn't finished yet, but I promise, you will be the first one to read it when I am all done." That was a close call. I will have to be more careful. Perhaps the next time she will have time to read it before I notice it is gone.

Later, I hear Ala's sneaky little feet walking down the hall, passing over the squeak in the floor. She sticks her head in the kitchen doorway and says, "Only eleven days until your daddy gets here."

What?

Auntie says, "I received the letter from your Dad this morning. I meant to talk to you about it, but I plumb forgot earlier. He asked if we could keep you for a little while longer until he finishes with some of the farm chores. He would like to come on August twenty-second to pick you up. Is that alright with you?"

"Yes, thank you, Auntie. That is fine with me." I think Ala must be happy to know she will be getting rid of me. And maybe that is why over the next few days Ala and I become closer. We talk about boys a lot, chase butterflies and share all the chores. We collect honey from the hives near the bushes and tell each other stories of our futures.

I look forward to each new day and what it will bring. I don't ever want to end this part of my journey. I don't want my time here to end, I tell myself every day.

But I still keep a close watch over my notebook.

Chapter Thirty-One

I know I have promised my auntie that I will stay away from Michael, but today he asks, "Let's go to the gravel pit. A few friends from my school will be there for a small party in the dugout."

I am honored and excited that Michael is asking me to come with him. I have never been invited to a party before as I am too young and not very popular.

I remember my Grandma Kula always calls me her smart, beautiful girl, but she is my grandma after all and she is supposed to say things like that. Often I look at my skinny body in the tall mirror that stands on Auntie's floor, trying to figure out what needs to be fixed. My eyes are very blue, and I have a nice smile, but I have a flat chest. "What boy would want to look at me?" I keep thinking.

I tell Michael, "I am not sure I want to go." I don't have any party clothes. Inside, I am dying to meet his friends and be part of his group. I am also thinking that when Auntie finds out, she won't let us go anyways.

Michael says, "What do you mean, you are not sure?" He seems disappointed. I want him to like me and I want to feel special.

"What if your friends laugh at me?" I couldn't bear it.

Auntie Veronica hears us discussing this party, and she asks Michael a lot of questions about it. After pondering a while, she announces, "The only way you two can go to the gravel pit party is if Ala goes with you. She will keep her eyes on things."

Michael groans. "Oh no, not my baby sister as a chaperone."

"Either Ala goes," says Auntie, "or no party for you two."

As the three of us approach the gravel pit, a couple of boys from Michael's school are flicking lit matches at each other and laughing. A few of them are passing around a thick cigarette. I hope Michael will not be part of that.

"Where did you get the cigarette?" Michael asks one of the boys.

"John stole it from his dad," Victor says. The boys are all yelling and laughing and flicking their matches everywhere.

Ala's eyes are as big as saucers and she says, "I am going home."

I get Michael's attention. "I don't want to go to the dugout."

Michael takes my hand. "Don't worry, it will be alright."

Slowly we approach his friends. An old wagon is propped up on three wheels. Its metal parts are all rusty, and there is an old, broken box sitting on top of it.

The boys are swarming all over the wagon, chasing each other with lit matches and flicking them everywhere. Then I smell smoke. A fire starts to crackle and suddenly with a loud boom pieces of the wagon come flying toward us.

The next thing I know, I am on the ground and Auntie Veronica is looking down at me with her neighbor, Nicholas. The other boys gone.

"What happened?" Auntie asks. Both her hands are propped on her hips, and she looks very angry.

Michael mumbles, "I don't know."

"Are you alright, Krysia?" she asks. As I turn, she gasps. "You are hurt."

My head does hurt, and when I put my hand on my face, it is very sore. I can feel blood running down by face, and I can't see through my left eye. I start to cry. "Oh, no, I lost my eye," I scream.

"No, no," says Nicholas. "You will be fine."

I feel lightheaded. Nicholas picks me up and carries me home. Auntie Veronica puts some sticky stuff around my eye and I fall asleep.

Later, when I wake up, everyone is staring at me.

Auntie Veronica asks, "Are you alright?"

"I think I am fine," I squeak. "I don't really hurt anywhere, except for my forehead."

"We are glad you are okay," says Auntie.

"I don't remember what happened," I mumble.

Michael says, "When the wood flew toward us, you backed up and tripped on a rock and hit your head."

"It could have been much worse," says Auntie Veronica. I know she is concerned or frightened for me, and I thank God for being with me and protecting me from any more danger.

&~ ~&

One day while Michael and Ala are away visiting friends on their farm outside the city, Auntie and I are sitting on the bed talking about my family when suddenly she is sick. I help her lie back. Her face is the color of the pale walls behind her headboard and her eyes are glossy. She moans and groans as she turns from side to side, and I hear her starting to pray. I know when Mom starts to pray it is usually really, really bad. I tell her to relax and keep praying, and I will run to the neighbors for some help.

Mrs. Jazek is an older lady, and she lives with her son who is often working out of town. He got Mrs. Jazek a telephone for any emergencies when he is not at home. When she answers her door, she recognizes me. "How nice of you to come and visit me," she says, but then she sees the frightened look on my face. "What's wrong child, are you alright?"

"Auntie is holding her chest and she is in a lot of pain" I gasp. "We need a doctor."

"I will call for Dr. Olewski," she says. "Go back to your auntie. He will be right there."

"Thank you, thank you." I dash out her front door.

When I approach Auntie's bed, I see tears in her eyes. "It's alright," I say. "You are going to be okay, please don't cry. The doctor is on his way." I sound calm and confident, but inside my heart is pounding.

I rinse a cloth in cold water and put it on Auntie's forehead. I hold it there and pray that it will help her. I do this often for my mom and she tells me it does help her a lot.

As we sit and wait, I feel tears spring up in my eyes and I worry what will happen to my auntie. That doctor is taking his sweet time getting here. Why is it taking so long? It seems hours since Mrs. Jazek called him; where is he?

Auntie is very still. Oh, Lord, please don't take her away from me. What if something bad is happening and the doctor takes her away to the hospital?

Finally there is a knock on the door and I almost trip running so fast to open it. "Please come in. She is lying down on her bed, but she doesn't look good."

"What happened?" the doctor asks.

I cover my eyes with my hands and start to cry. "We were talking and all of a sudden Auntie got some upset and was clenching her chest."

"Don't worry, she might have had a mild heart attack, or it could be something else," he says. "Now leave me to check her over." He closes the door in my face. There is nothing I can do now, except sit and wait and pray.

We had been talking about my life at home, and how I wish I could stay with Auntie, when she suddenly got so sick. What have I done? I caused this thing to happen.

I pace the floor in the kitchen area and I worry about what will happen if Auntie dies. "No, no, the doctor may only have to take Auntie to the hospital for a while, until she gets stronger," I assure myself. Either way, I am sure this means I will be on my way back home tomorrow.

Dr. Olewski walks out and closes the door behind him. "You make sure she takes her medicine, and she is to be very still and quiet for the next few days. No one is to upset her. I will hold you responsible for that," he says as he heads out the front door.

"I will, I will look after my auntie," I say, shaking.

After he leaves, I feel like jumping for joy. Auntie will be alright. "Thank you, Lord, for answering my prayers," I say out loud.

All I know now is that I am glad that Michael and Ala were not here to witness this upsetting incident. And I am glad I have a few more hours to calm down and spend time helping Auntie to get stronger before they get home. I will make her a cup of tea and some soup.

A moaning noise is coming from the bedroom. I go running and see that Auntie is awake. "What can I get for you?" I ask.

"Water, water," she is straining to say. When I hold the glass to her lips, she looks pale and weak and I feel terrible. She leans back on her pillow and closes her eyes, and I wait and wait for her to wake up, but she sleeps for a long time. Exhausted, I finally fall asleep, and I don't even hear Michael and Ala come home.

The next morning, Auntie is the first one in the kitchen getting things ready for breakfast. She looks quite pale, but she is smiling as though nothing happened. She puts an arm around my shoulders and asks me to promise not to tell anyone she has been sick.

I promise. And I promise I will never upset her again. We will not talk about my life or our families. She means too much to me and is like a mother to me. I am very grateful to my auntie that she lets me stay here with them.

And I am waiting for August twenty-second to come, like a court date.

Chapter Thirty-Two

I awake to an announcement from Ala. "Your dad is coming tomorrow to get you, and you better be ready." I cover my head and have this sunken feeling in the bottom of my stomach. I don't want this adventure to end, not yet, not ever.

What will my dad do to me when he gets here? Maybe he'll say, "I am happy to see you," or "I am glad you had a chance to visit with your cousins." But I am not stupid; this trip has been stressful and costly for my parents, and they have been minus two helping hands all summer.

It is eating me up not knowing what he will do. Which dad will be here? I am hoping it will be the nice, gentle dad coming to get me, the one that looks at nature with wonder and beauty and amazing appreciation for life. I know it is too much to ask for, after all I have done, this unthinkable deed of running away from my responsibilities.

What will happen to me? How will this damage our relationship in the future?

I will worry more about that tomorrow.

༈ ༈

The day has come and Dad will be on the early evening train, just after supper. Auntie Veronica seems cooler toward me. I know deep down in her heart she does love me. She has told me many times these past weeks that I am her favorite niece.

Maybe she is worried about what Dad will do, too.

Eating supper is a chore for me today, as my stomach has been doing flipflops all day. My hands are sweating, I feel quite flushed, and my throat is dry. Afterward, I sit at the table quietly praying, "Dear God, make this meeting with my dad comfortable and take my fears away. I will be good and do things right from now on."

A loud knock at the front door scares me out of my wits. I know it is him, and I go to open the door. My chest is tight; there is darkness and ice all the way through me. I am shivering as my dad is standing in front of me. "Hi Dad," I say.

Every muscle wants to run to him, grab him in an embrace and tell him, "I am very sorry for running away." I study his face and wait for the signal. I don't want to make him angry with me. His eyes show disapproval.

"You should be hung by your fingernails." Dad walks in the door, and I back away. If looks could kill, I would be dead.

Then Auntie Veronica steps in front of me with her hands on her hips. "Jozef, come in and have some lemonade."

"Thank you, God, for sending Auntie to my rescue," I whisper under my breath.

I feel ice cold, as if something dangerous has slipped into the room. Everything has turned absolutely silent. I take a deep breath to steady myself and muster out again, "Hi Dad."

His boots clunk toward the kitchen table. He sits down and asks, "What am I going to do with you?"

I can't stand it any longer and I launch into him and tell him, "I love you, Daddy, and I missed you." I hold my breath and keep myself from crying.

Dad looks exhausted. He is wiping sweat off his forehead.

Auntie Veronica pours him some lemonade. "You have had a long journey," she says. "What time is your train going back tomorrow?"

"Early after lunch," Dad tells her.

Auntie looks relieved, "Well then, we have some time to visit and sort things out. Lie down and rest. We can talk in the morning."

Auntie points to the bed for Dad to lie down and closes the door behind him. She grabs my hand and pulls me toward the back door. "Come with me, we have many chores to finish," she says, as she almost drags me out.

At this time I am feeling protected and cared for and thinking how nice it would be if Auntie wanted to adopt me and I could stay here forever. I don't want to face my dad later, and I don't want to think about what is waiting for me at home.

Auntie seems to know what I'm thinking. "I pleaded with your dad in the telegram to give you a few weeks with us," she says as we finish up the chores. "I felt you needed this time to sort out what is important in your life. Also, you needed to be just a kid. My girl, you have never been young. You need to experience life as a child first before you become an adult." She looks at me with tears in her eyes and hugs me tight. "You can always come back here and find work when you grow up. For now, you need to go home and love your life, as it makes living much easier."

∂ ∽

The next day Auntie Veronica enters the bedroom. "Krysia, why aren't you packing? Your dad will be back shortly."

I have been looking out the window at Michael and Ala, and totally losing myself in the beauty of Auntie's colorful flowers. I have so little color in my life and I don't want this to end.

Auntie comes to stand behind me. I turn around and say, "I am just looking at the lawn and your beautiful garden and I will be haunted forever by the fact that I am leaving here. You are a kindred spirit, my auntie, someone I can rely on. I will miss our talks and life's lessons, and I look forward to seeing you when you come visit us in Topola."

Auntie Veronica hugs me tight. "Keep writing in your journal about the bees and the butterflies and other stuff you like. One day you might be a famous writer."

I nod. Everything that happened to me, the good and the bad, is more than I can make up. "Maybe one day I will write about my visit here."

Dad is back from visiting a school friend and sees we are crying. "What's all the fuss about?" He is still upset with me and I can hear it in his voice. I am not looking forward to our long train trip. I know I have hurt him a lot, and I don't know how I'll ever regain his trust. The only thing I can do is pray for his forgiveness.

"Goodbyes are never fun," says Auntie Veronica. "I have really enjoyed having you here, Krysia. We will miss you and your adventures around here. It will never be the same without you."

"I will never forget you, my favorite auntie," I tell her.

Michael and Ala come in, and we all start hugging and crying and saying our goodbyes. "I will miss you, my cousins, and the fun times we've had. I'll be thinking about you guys often until our next visit."

And then, too soon, my time with them is done.

Chapter Thirty-Three

Dad and I are walking down the same long street to the train station. He doesn't say a word and keeps striding along, carrying my suitcase. I am practically running behind him all the way down the hill.

I see the sun spreading across the sky, setting the tops of buildings on fire, and the ground begins to get darker. The heat seems to build up in the skies and over the whole city. Finally, as we approach the train station, a clap of thunder rumbles, lightning flashes, and rain begins pouring down.

The train is on time, so we don't have to wait long. It is very uncomfortable to see Dad's disappointed and angry face. I am still afraid and I am not looking forward to this trip together. After getting ourselves seated and showing our tickets to the conductor, we are left all alone in the train car.

Here it goes, now I am going to get it. "Oh Lord, help me out and give Dad compassion toward me." Every time he looks at me, I feel so guilty for running away and for hurting him like that.

Finally I reach out and touch his hand. It is a large, hard-working hand, and full of calluses. I miss those hands that held mine when we went for our walks together in the past. I hope we can do that again once we are home.

Dad turns around from staring out the window, and I can see the sadness in his big blue eyes. Tears come to my eyes and I blurt out, "I am very sorry for running away, and I promise I'll never do that again. Please forgive me, Daddy, for hurting you and Mom like this."

His eyes get cloudy with tears, and after a moment he finally gives me a tight hug. He holds me close to him for what seems like an hour as we both tremble in silence.

"You could have been kidnapped or abused or killed and thrown in the ditch somewhere and we would have never found you. What were you thinking?"

I think, "He is on the way to forgiveness. Thank you, Lord."

"The most frightening thing of all is that you could have ended just about anywhere," he continues. "How would we have been able to find you? You are too young to have any sense of direction, and yet you did find Auntie's place in the middle of the night. How, how on earth did you find her place? Did someone bring you there? Weren't you frightened to travel all by yourself? What were you thinking when you decided to leave home? Was it that bad living with us?" He wipes his tears and blows his nose and shakes his head.

I don't like how these questions make me feel.

I cannot stop him now. "We searched the whole town with all our relatives, who make up about half the town, and all your friends and classmates, and no one had heard from you or seen you. How did you walk through the whole town to the train station dragging this suitcase without anyone noticing you?"

I am crying, and I don't know how to answer my dad.

"When we didn't hear from you, we assumed the worst. Every moment that passed meant that you could be getting picked up by a stranger and being talked into who knows what. Why did you wait so long to contact us? It would have helped at least to know where you were."

Sniffling, I answer, "I didn't want you to come and get me right away. I begged Auntie Veronica to let me stay for a few days before contacting you."

"Your Mom felt so helpless. The possibility of losing another child could have put her over the edge. Why did you do this to us? We didn't know if we were going to find you, or if we should be making funeral plans. All we had left was to pray, pray, and pray more for your safety and we kept asking everyone else to pray as well."

While Dad is going on and on about how I have hurt them, I feel small, like the dust on my shoes. I am listening and nodding and I am trying to show Dad how sorry I am. I am not looking forward to getting home to more lectures. I don't think I can feel any worse than I am feeling right now.

The trip drags along and I don't say much at all. I want to tell him how I enjoyed my time with Auntie Veronica and my cousins. How I learned a lot about the bees and the rabbits and how God loves us all without judgement. So many things I want to tell him, but looking at him I realize he needs to be the one to talk.

Finally the conductor announces, "Here's your stop. Have a nice evening." He tips his hat toward us.

I swallow hard and keep my head down.

Dad grabs and squeezes my hand as we step off the train. Then he turns around to face me. His anger fades some and he says, "I will never let you go again."

We walk all the way home without saying another word. The warmth of his hand is somewhat comforting. I continue to pray under my breath for a peaceful reunion with my family.

As we approach our house, Mom runs outside. "Thank you, dear Lord." She gives me the tightest hug I've ever had from her. She holds me in her arms for what seem like hours and keeps repeating, "I'll never, ever let you go anywhere, ever again."

Oh, boy. Mom had started spying on me wherever I went before I ran away, and now she will be glued to me. I'll just have to stay busy all the time.

I have come home sheepishly, expecting everyone's disapproval, but instead I get a big welcome from Mom, my brothers and my grandparents. I know this is not over and the punishment is forthcoming.

After the hugging and tears from everyone have subsided, Dad tells me, "Your chores are waiting for you and it is best you get back to them."

Before walking away to resume his chores, Dad turns around and looks at me again. "Don't you do anything stupid like that ever again, you hear."

I promise by nodding my head, but inside I am dying. Same old chores, same old rules, and nothing will ever change.

Mom looks at me so happily and says, "I am so glad you are alright and that nothing bad has happened to you. You better do what your dad says."

I am glad that Mom was able to cope without me these past two months. She looks very tired, but she has not stopped smiling at me since I got home. I know she missed me very much.

I tell brother Stan, "Looks like you have grown some."

At nine years old, he seems older and I know he has been working hard alongside our father. He smiles at me and says,

"You are lucky you didn't get a spanking with Dad's new leather belt. It really hurts a lot more than the old beat-up one."

Jim is now seven, and is doing more chores too. He looks at me with his sad eyes and says, "I am glad you are home, Sister," before going to feed our chickens.

Grandma holds me tight to her chest without saying a word and I can hear her heart beat. Grandpa shrugs his shoulders and says, "Oh, you finally made it home. I had to string my tobacco leaves by myself this summer, you know." That tobacco is very important to him and I have let him down as well.

I am aware that I still have to face up to the rumors about Tomek and me. I still feel the same about him, but for now, I am not sure what will happen with us. I have changed over the summer. I have different ideas to implement into my life, and I have no choice but to make the best out of this life on our farm.

Finally I go to say hello to Babunia, our milking cow, and she turns her head to look at me and moos. I choose to think that she is welcoming me home. I pick up the pail, sit on the three-legged stool, and gently start pulling on her teats until milk starts to come. I smile to myself and think that my dream of a better life is not over, so I might as well enjoy what I am doing right now.

I adapt quickly to my old life and settle back in my space behind the tall dresser. Everything here is just as I left it.

On Sunday Dad announces, "We are going to visit my relatives after church. They live two kilometers from the church toward the hills. My cousin is not well and I would like to see him before anything happens."

My dad's father has ten siblings and all together they have thirty-two children, which makes thirty-two cousins for my dad. Most of them live out of town, spread all over the hills. But we have visited mostly with my dad's relatives on his mom's side. Grandma has thirteen siblings. That makes forty-seven cousins on her side. Lots of them live close by, so we get to see more of them and have gotten to know them better.

I don't remember ever going to visit with Grandpa's relatives. Maybe Dad wants me to have more cousins to visit that live closer to us, who are also closer to my age. "Do they have any kids our ages?" I ask.

Dad says, "They do have two boys, but I am not sure how old they are."

We hurry with breakfast, get dressed and are on our way to church, singing gospel songs to pass the time.

Once in a while I get that look from my dad. He is still very disappointed in me. I know I have to earn his trust again and I will not give him any cause to mistrust me.

I am looking forward to meeting our new cousins and having some fun. I miss Ala and Michael and all the adventures we had. I miss those warm hugs from Auntie Veronica, and her wisdom. I will keep those memories in my heart forever.

After the church service is over, we gather together and start walking to Uncle Bart's place. The winding, uphill gravel road is hard to walk on. Loose gravel is getting into my sandals and hurting my feet.

"My foot is bleeding, Dad," I say.

"Stop whining," he says. "We are just about there."

Auntie Barbara answers the door. "Come in, come in and have a seat. Bart is lying down; he is not feeling well."

Inside the house is nice and clean, with a large table and many chairs—a welcome sight after the grueling trip on that rocky road. Something on the stove smells good, and Auntie's kind smile is very inviting. She sees that I am limping. "What have we here, my girl? You are bleeding. Let me look at it." She takes my sandal off and finds a sharp rock that was grinding into my toe. "We will put a bandage on that. After lunch, you will be able to go and play with your cousins. They will be home soon."

Dad and Mom have gone to the other room where Uncle Bart is, and they are visiting with him. I can hear some laughter coming from the bedroom. My uncle's deep voice says, "I haven't laughed like this since forever. I am glad you guys are here."

Auntie returns with the bandage. The door opens and two tall boys walk in. "There you are." My auntie introduces us. "This is our oldest son, Adam, and our youngest, Jurek."

Adam says, "I am pleased to make your acquaintance, Cousins," as he shakes hands with me, and with Stan and Jim. Jurek stretches his hand out to each of us and says, "Me too."

Auntie announces, "Now that we are all together we will have lunch. I will get Bart and your parents to come and join us. You boys set the table."

Watching my cousins set the table is a treat. It is usually my job at home.

After our prayers, we have soup with fresh buns straight from the oven and get to know one another. Then the boys wash the dishes and I dry them.

I like being with my cousins, especially with Adam. Dad suggests, "You kids go outside and feed the chickens and keep busy for a while; we want to visit with the adults."

The sun is high and it is very warm. My brothers are running around chasing chickens with our cousin Jurek and screaming at each other. Adam says, "Come, I want to show you our swing under the plum tree in the back yard. It is much cooler there in the shade." The swing is made out of shiny wood and is big enough for two people. The shade from the plum tree is lovely.

We sit down and start swinging gently back and forth. Adam asks me, "What grade are you going into?"

"Grade seven," I tell him. "What grade are you going into?"

"Grade nine," he answers. "What did you do this summer?"

"Well, I went away to visit our cousins in Sosnoviec until last week. It was a great trip."

"You went all by yourself? That is a long ways. How did your parents agree to let you go by yourself?"

"Well . . ."

I am thinking about how to answer when I hear some noise coming from the next-door neighbor's yard, and I go to the fence to see what it is.

Oh my God.

It is Ed.

He is unloading his wagon, and I drop down so he will not see me behind the fence.

Adam has followed me to the fence and he asks, "What is the matter?"

I cannot tell him. What am I going to do? I have to think fast and say something, but what?

"Are you hurt?" Adam asks.

I am shaking and afraid that Ed will spot me, so I say, "No, I am fine."

Adam pulls me to my feet, and I glance over to see if Ed has seen me. He has. Now he is standing against his side of the fence, looking at me. "My, my, look who's here. I told you we would meet again, but I didn't think it would be this soon."

"Do you know each other?" Adam asks.

I am very anxious to leave, and I tug at my cousin's sleeve. "Let's go to the barn to see your animals."

Ed has that same smirk on his face. "Yes, we are old friends from way back. I didn't know you guys are related."

"Come on, Adam," I say as I grab his hand. "Let's go see the animals before I have to leave for home."

From behind us, Ed says, "We will be seeing each other very soon. We can finish what we started two months ago, you can count on that."

In the barn I am shaking and stammering. Adam asks, "What was that all about it? How do you know him? What is he going to finish with you?"

"He is crazy. He gave me a ride in his wagon from our farm road to Topola two months ago and scared me to death. I don't ever want to see him again. Does he live next door?"

"Yes," says Adam. "He lived there with his mom until about a month ago, when she passed away. Now he lives there by himself. We don't have much to do with him. Most people don't like him very much."

A shudder runs through me. Ed lives all alone, so he has no one to answer to. I am afraid he might use our cousins to find me. I don't know Adam well enough to tell him about everything that happened. And I am afraid to tell my parents. I have caused enough trouble for them.

の の

As we begin the long walk home, Dad announces, "I have been thinking. Perhaps we should get to work on moving to Canada, like Grandpa Janiga suggested in his last letter. It will take a couple of years to get ready, and to sell our farm. We may find life a bit easier over there, but it won't be free."

Mom is very excited. "I will be able to meet my dad for the first time, and see my mom again. I miss her. She has been gone for so long."

Dad promises, "One way or another, we will get out of this Godforsaken town. Today, let's say our prayers and be grateful for having Krystyna back home."

I will pray every day that we will go to Canada soon. In the meantime, I am happy to have new cousins to think about. I feel like I can take care of myself because I am older now, and I have traveled and have new ideas in my head. But tomorrow, my parents will be going to the farm for the day and we will be alone in the house after school. Will Ed find me? I know that worrying about him will cast a dark shadow over all my days.

I am hoping that things will soon change for the better. Dad has promised to look into moving to Canada. As long as I have something to look forward to, I will work and sing and stay content.

About the Author

Krystyna Bellamy grew up in a farming community in Poland and started taking notes on everything around her from the time she was five years old. As a young teen she immigrated with her family to Canada, where she has worked in the corporate world in training and management for many years.

Each opportunity in her life has shaped her view of the world and sparked yet another journey into more curiosity—and more writing, especially adventure and drama.

When she is not glued to a computer screen, Krystyna spends time reading, painting, skiing, golfing, and going for long walks.